What's on the Menu?

O'RESEA MITCHELL

ISBN: 978-0-9978719-0-6

I dedicate this book to my beautiful daughter, who has been and I'm sure will always be my personal cheerleader. I thank God that He has blessed me with an independent, smart, funny, positive, bubbly, energetic and loving little girl who never ceases to amaze me. I pray that God continues to favor your life, and to give you the knowledge, strength and wisdom to be a young woman who loves Him first, loves yourself and walks in the anointing that He has placed on your life. Anna-Bear I love you! May you know the beauty and joy of one day saving yourself specifically for the one man God has reserved just for you!

To my husband, yes, I dedicate this book to you too! I cannot wait; I mean I can, but not too much longer, to finally meet you as my man! Wink! I thank God for you in advance by doing what comes natural; covering you with my prayers. I'm preparing myself to be the woman who is deserving of the man that you are, by realizing that you too will have done or are doing the same. You are 100% right for me, and I couldn't ask God for anything greater. God knew since the foundation of the world that we two imperfect people would be amazingly perfect together, and that is what keeps me motivated to wait patiently.

And finally, to you, all God's beautiful and amazing women! Don't be discouraged because it hasn't happened. Realize that greater blessings require more time to manifest, and that being single is more of an opportunity for the favor of God to be selfishly wrought in your lives!

Contents

Introduction

————✦————

I t's true. There are many Christian women (and men for that matter) struggling in their walk with God as "singles." Our struggle (I'm in the same single boat as you) is not because we don't love God, and for some, it's not that we don't trust Him. This struggle is not necessarily because we are doing something wrong. God has brought it to my attention that in this struggle of being "single," it's only a struggle because we don't understand His unique design of marriage.

"That is not true," someone reading this book will say or think within their mind. A handful of readers will say that because they've been married before and they understand what God's unique design of marriage is. How do they know what it is? They know because they've been married. However, and this is not meant to chastise, but to simply drop some knowledge, if you knew what God's plan for marriage was, would you have gotten divorced? Let's take it a step further; would you have gotten married to that person originally? Deep right? Not really, but --really. God requires us to go beyond the surface. So, yes, it is deep, just not that deep.

This brings me to the woman who has never been married and believes that she understands God's unique design of marriage. Now how is that possible? Your understanding comes from the fact that you've read every Christian book on marriage, completed every devotional, fasted and prayed, however, to no avail, you yet find yourself in a place of lack (being single), according to you that is.

Ha! That isn't to laugh in your face. Beautiful and anointed women of God, it's laughing with you. As I'm writing this book, I'm also in your position. I'm just grateful that God has shed some light on me to share with you all. According to Matthew 5:16 (KJV), I am to "Let your light so shine before men, that they see your works, and glorify your Father which is in heaven." As I let the light of God shine through me, know that God cannot fulfill Himself in our lives if we don't acknowledge Him as the source of our everything! What do I mean? God cannot satisfy or meet our spiritual and physical needs if we do not recognize that God is the source of what we need.

God has given me a glimpse of how our relationship with Him is in fact preparation for marriage. Are we not the Bride (the church), and Jesus the Bridegroom? We are! Establishing a relationship with God for a spiritual marriage where our souls are eternally connected with His, is preparation for a physical marriage where we are united to a man.

There are already some women by this point who are skeptical of what lies ahead. I encourage you, however, to open your heart and your mind to receive something great from God. God desires to have an intimate relationship with you. This is why He sent His son Jesus, who He loved, to die for us, whom He loved more! Isn't that amazing? God so openly and willingly sacrificed His only begotten son He loved, and in whom He was well pleased, that each and every one of us could have life. Not only did God love us that much, but also Jesus being God in the flesh had the power of choice. He chose us! Why not enter into an intimate relationship with them? We have to accept Jesus as our personal (intimate) Lord and Savior. He is the door, and through Him we have access to the Father. Just thinking about this gets me all excited! What about you?

Does the love God has for you make you excited? If not, answer this one question; as a Christian woman, how can the love that a man offers you make you feel any better or different? Now that's deep! It can't make you feel better and it won't make you feel different. You'll always feel unfulfilled, as though you are lacking "fireworks," or the magical fairytale feeling if you as a Christian woman haven't accepted and embraced the love God has for you.

I was totally convicted when God gave me this book to write. Convicted because I felt unworthy. I've been one to seek out love in all the wrong places. I've searched for validation or approval (i.e. the need to be loved) from men, when my Heavenly father has had all that I needed. I've read the books that are supposed to prepare you for marriage, I've done the devotionals, I've prayed and cried, but this small revelation has been working wonders in my life. God is my source and He is my everything! Until we can understand

and experience a true, intimate relationship with God, His unique design of marriage will be foreign to us.

We are going to explore how God has a unique design of marriage more deeply than God's plan for marriage. "Of" and "for" are both prepositions; however, they describe the relation that God has to marriage in two different ways. Most of the time we hear about how God has a plan for marriage; meaning "marriage" has a purpose or function. As it relates to the will of God, marriage does have a purpose and a function. To function means there are working parts, a husband and a wife. However, that does not benefit those of us who are single. We cannot function in something that has no relevance to our current status. This is why we deal with God's unique design of marriage--of, being a preposition expressing the relationship between a part and a whole.

I am a part of the body of Christ. The body is made up of many parts or members. Together, we make a whole. Once we understand what we contribute as a part, we can function as a whole. Do you see where this is going? Until we understand our relationship to God and what He has for our lives, we will not be able to understand the function marriage will serve in our lives.

I am both ecstatic and jubilant. We are embarking on a journey from this point on (oh yes! I speak that thang), that will have us seeking the face of God, allowing us to be triumphant. No longer will we seek Him only for His blessings, without dedication; but we will now begin to establish real and fulfilling relationships with the lover of our soul. Here is my prayer for you,

Dear most gracious and heavenly father,

I thank you for the women that are reading this book. It is not by chance that they have it in their hands now. You divinely orchestrate everything according to the love you have toward us. For that, I give you thanks. For there is truly no one like you, anywhere! God, you have given me such a great word to share with these beautiful women, because you see our need for comfort, for love, companionship, validation, and for sweet nothings to be whispered in our ear. Your desire oh Lord, is that we find comfort in your arms, that we love you as you love us. God, show us true companionship.

Validate our lives by gracing us with your presence, power, and Holy Spirit. God, you be the sweet nothings in our ear. God, allow our hunger and desire for you to captivate our hearts and minds. Help us to rely on you as the source of our everything. Heal the hurting heart. Restore joy and peace where the enemy has brought sorrow and desolation. You are our portion! Strengthen us where we have become weak. Teach us to treat ourselves with respect. Show us how to love us. Show us how to appreciate this temple you've created us to be. Oh God, do in us a new and a great thing. You are the potter and we are the clay. God, mold us to be the women you created us to be. We will be living epistles read of men. We will give you glory, and we will give you honor. We will exalt you father, for you alone are worthy! You are worthy oh God, for us to submit ourselves unto you. Worthy that we become vessels of honor, fit for your use. We are precious jewels, the apple of your eye and I declare now that the struggle IS OVER! We are victorious! Thank you for all that you are. In Jesus name, I pray. Amen!

I have faith enough to believe that God is more than able to do exceedingly and abundantly above what we ask or think. However, we have to position ourselves to be recipients. I look forward to all the testimonies that will arise from this journey that you will embark upon with God. Be blessed!

Chapter

1

A Part to A Whole

As a Christian, you are a vital part of the body of Christ. As an individual, you serve a unique purpose in the body.

Lately, I've been hearing a lot of talk about living with purpose, or walking in your destiny. There is a resounding message about the disconnection from knowing what purpose you serve, and fulfilling that purpose. The messages are to seek God to discover what your purpose is. Why is that?

Have you ever been in a situation where you felt as though you were the only one working, and there was still so much that had to be done? So did Jesus! In Matthew 9 (KJV) in verse 36, it talks about how Jesus was moved with compassion on them, being the multitude. Verse 37 reads, "Then saith he unto his disciples, The harvest truly is plenteous, but the labourers are few;" verse 38 "Pray ye therefore the Lord of the harvest, that he will send forth labourers into his harvest."

This chapter is a vital part of this book, which is why it is first! Please stick with me. As my pastor, Pastor Thomas, would say, I'm building my train.

God keeps giving people the messages to give to us that we need to walk in our purpose and destiny, because there is a harvest, and God has sent US! God is sending us as "labourers," to work in His field or vineyards. We have something that this world needs. God has instilled within us the panacea for someone's healing, and the words of encouragement for someone's deliverance.

As Christians, our circumstances often distract us to the point that we don't realize that those same circumstances are the tools we need to glean! Your testimony is someone else's deliverance! It hurts! I know that it does. But eventually you'll have to open your mouth and use that to help somebody. Therefore, we cannot afford to get thrown off the path set before us when circumstances arise. I get it. It's easier said than done. However, realize that your life is not your own, and it was meant to help somebody else.

Women of God, before our life can function in a marriage, it has to function as a part to a whole!

As a baby develops from birth, before it can walk, talk, run, and explore the world, it explores its body in parts. This exploration is considered to be milestones. Their hands easily amaze them. Eventually, that baby is mastering the use of their hands. It has reached a milestone that enables the infant to understand the function of his or her hands in relation to its survival.

Just as us, we have to understand gradually what function we serve in the body of Christ! Before we explore and function, we need to reach the proper milestones. Circumstances, trials, sickness, frustration, fear, doubt, addictions, bad relationships and whatever else the devil may have meant for evil, are all meant to help us in our role as "labourers."

You may ask, "what does that have to do with me one day entering into a marriage?" EVERYTHING!

Way back when our great-grandparents and grandparents were getting married, they were raised to love God first. Now, WE love us and then want someone else to love us, and we leave whatever we have left for God. That doesn't work for God.

The reason we've been waiting for a mate for so long, is because God has to recondition our thinking, our attitudes and our habits. We've forgotten trivial things. We were meant to glorify God, not God glorify us! We are laborers for God. God doesn't work for us.

WE have forgotten the first marriage didn't happen right away either.

Adam was active in ministry before Eve was ever introduced to him. Before Adam noticed his lack, that is his uniqueness in being single, he was working!

Genesis 2:8 (KJV) "And the Lord God planted a garden eastward in Eden; and there he put the man whom he formed." Verse 15, " And the Lord God took the man, and put him into the garden of Eden to dress it and keep it." Verse 19, " And out of the ground the Lord God formed every beast of the field, and every fowl of the air; and brought them unto Adam to see what he would call them: and whatsoever Adam called every living creature, that was the name thereof."

Say what? Adam was doing what God told him to do? Adam was functioning in the capacity for which God created him, to have dominion! Hmm? As I am writing, it is amazing how things are yet falling into place to make sense and how this small thing we overlook often, is a great revelation to our current situation. HA! I'm absolutely tickled!

We've been waiting because we haven't been working! This is something we've considered to be negligible, but in fact, it is of great importance. God is not going to allow you to enter into a marriage that serves a function if you can't even work as a part to a whole.

To reword this in a way that brings it all together, as single people our struggle is ultimately not because God doesn't desire to see us happy naturally. As Christians, we are struggling with being single because we are attempting to function in a capacity in which we cannot relate. We are trying to figure out why we're not married, and God is trying to figure out why we're not working! I've heard many married women say, 'get busy for God, and before you know it, the right one will be here.'

Too much valuable time is being spent on seeking marriage, when we have a ripe harvest waiting on us. We are attempting to do things out of order. As we should know, God is a God of order.

I had an issue with this. Being transparent, I used to think, "God, how did you allow Brother Maple and Sister Syrup to get married? She isn't working like I'm working. Sister Syrup isn't even involved in ministry like I am or as I desire to be." God has revealed in so many different ways that I cannot compare what God has called me to do, with what He has called Mr. and Mrs. Maple Syrup to do.

My assignments are not anyone else's. My anointing is not your anointing. We may possess the same gifts, but we've been called to operate within them at different capacities.

We all serve a different function as a part in this whole body of Christ! Are you working? If so, are you working in the magnitude by which God has called you?

To bring this chapter to a logical close, let us consider what it means to work in the magnitude and capacity by which God has called you. Capacity is fully occupying the available area or space. Magnitude is the great size or extent of something. In essence, God is asking, "are you fully occupying the great area to the extent of which I have created and called you to?" Wow! Are you fully exercising the gifts God has placed inside of you to the best of your ability?

As a part of the body of Christ, are you first functioning to support the whole body? Not simply supporting your needs and desires, but the desire of the head, which is Christ. The body has to function as a whole, and in order to function, each individual part needs to function at its capacity according to the magnitude by which God is pleased. We can find this in 1 Corinthians 12. I encourage you to take a few minutes to grab your Bible and read it.

I am in awe of God right now. We all should be able to close the book from here and be better than okay. From this point, I declare that each individual who was able to grasp the revelation just from this chapter alone begins to find herself working at capacity! If by chance you missed it, I pray that God opens your understanding to the profoundness of this revelation, and that by doing so, you too begin to work at capacity.

Chapter

2

An Encounter With the King

———⁕———

G od is amazing! In writing this book, I've learned that God is not a God based on our logical computation of how things ought to work or flow. Because He is God, He does things the way that He desires.

When I was trying to figure out how this book should flow, I became stuck. However, as I acknowledged God, I found His rhythm and it all makes sense.

By chapter two, I figured I'd be getting deep into analogies of the book title, but God brought it to my awareness that at this juncture, it would lose its effectiveness! By building up to that chapter, it gives you, the reader, the foundation and understanding of why God has inspired this message for us.

In the previous chapter, it was mentioned how God is simply wondering why we aren't working. Why aren't we functioning at the capacity and magnitude by which He has called us? Why aren't we living on purpose and with purpose?

God's answer to me, "you haven't had a real encounter with me." What? God, what do you mean by encounter? If you are anything like me, you'd think, "I pray, I go to church, I study your word, God, I've spoken your word, and God, I'm seeking your face as best as I know how. God, you've filled me with your precious spirit, and I have the evidence. So, God, please clarify what you mean by real encounter?"

Have you ever known someone for years and one day, you two were talking as though you've never talked before and you learned something that you never knew before? In today's society, we have become so superficial in relationships that we fail to really get to know people, let alone know our God in a way that He desires.

I'm not saying you're fake, and God is not saying you're fake. Just ponder upon it. We've been in all types of relationships. Friends have come and gone, relationships with significant others have failed, family members have turned their backs on us, and we have disappointed ourselves. To avoid further disappointment, we laden ourselves with reminders of the disappointment, and only seek to know people superficially. We don't think we do, but we carry that baggage with us in our attempts to establish an everlasting relationship with God, our king!

We hide behind anger, frustration, disappointment, bitterness, and we enter into a relationship with God thinking He doesn't see our wounds. We therefore hold back from allowing ourselves from being free in Him!

I was in prayer one morning, and God as clear as day says, "I want you to let go. Give me all of you that you are still holding onto." Without attempt, I've been putting on a front with God. I talk to God about everything, but there is some baggage in my life that has been buried deep within the basements of my heart, and it weighs on me and causes me not to have a genuine encounter with God.

You, reading this book, what are you attempting to hide? Never mind the fact that you too have the evidence of His Holy Spirit. There are greater levels of intimacy in God that we cannot experience if we are not real with God.

Let's make the playing field even. We are all serving God at surface level! There is so much of each and every one of us that we haven't given or yielded completely over to God. You in fact may love God with everything within you, but you love your mother too. There are some things you have never told your mother. There are some things you've never addressed with God!

There are wounds that you figured time will heal and it's been nineteen years and you are still hurting. You've matured in Christ, but you still find yourself struggling with something you thought you were delivered from.

Why is that? Have we forgotten that our God is sovereign? Have we forgotten that God is not a man or a woman but a spirit?

We fear that if we expose the wounds to the only one who can heal us, that the only one who can comfort us will hurt us! That's insane- but it's true!

We have equated God with man on so many fronts, that in our surface relationships with Him, we can never truly become intimate with God because of fear. We not only hold our future husbands accountable for how someone else has treated us, but we hold God accountable.

God is not that man that abused you or the one that walked out on you. God is not that father that never availed himself to you. He is not that mother that gave you up because her wants and desires were more important. God is not that friend that betrayed your trust.

God is the creator of everything, and before He formed you in the womb of your mother, He had thoughts of you! I've shared this with so many different people, but years ago God encouraged me by letting me know that His thoughts of me were not good enough. He loved the thought of me so much that God had to put me into creation. That's powerful!

God loves you so much, that the thought of you was not enough. I'm not saying His thoughts weren't good, but not good enough. The thought of you did not satiate Him, so God had to create you. Have you ever been thinking about something and you just had to share it because it wasn't enough just for you to know? God was not satisfied until everything He has ever created knew that you were something special to Him.

That, in essence, is the love story of the Bible!

On Facebook, I shared something that will reiterate this point. Part of it read;

> ...the amount of thought that God has given to creating this earth in which He has given us dominion is great, and the thought He gave into creating us is even greater. So much so, that His thoughts of us were not good enough. His desire to show us His love was His driving force, His motivation, His inspiration to making us more than just His thoughts, but a reality. So He CREATED US! And in His intricate plan to show us His unconditional love, He has given us the assurance in Jeremiah 29:11 that His thoughts for us in fact have not changed, but are thoughts of peace and not evil.

God being omniscient knew that there would be a time in our lives that we would face circumstances, difficulties… that would cause us to be bold enough to question Him as to why or to what purpose the different things that arise in our life served. So He had to let us know none of this was from "*evil*" thoughts, but a place of love and peace. He is in fact creating situations, allowing circumstances, difficulties… He is permitting the enemy to wreak havoc… as a means to prove that His love is in fact unconditional and that it is peculiar to us. For why then being just a little bit lower than the angels would He visit us, while they sit in His presence saying Holy! Holy! Holy! There is an aspect of God's love that supersedes the love He has for any other being (i.e. angelic), to where He would come Himself in sinful flesh as the 'begotten,' and die for us that we may live, that we may know His love!

Everything has been divinely orchestrated according to the love God has for you! We don't see things that way because we don't view life through the lens of love. Love is spiritual not carnal. This is why we need to experience the love of God the father first, before attempting to enter into a marriage where we think we know what love is.

It is only through a real and divine encounter with God that we can learn and embrace the love God has for us! Before we discuss how you can have a real encounter with God, let's explore who God is.

Exodus 3:14 (KJV) "And God said unto Moses, I AM THAT I AM: and he said, Thus shalt thou say unto the children of Israel, I AM hath sent me unto you." God is! God is the great "I AM." Do you recognize how powerful that statement is? God is self-sustaining and self-sufficient. I AM can be all you need because of who He is!

God is infinite. This means that God is both limitless and endless. Revelation 1:8 (KJV) "I am Alpha and Omega, the beginning and the ending, saith the Lord, which is, and which was, and which is to come, the Almighty." God is always God. There is no end to Him. Therefore, He has existed from your birth and will exist beyond your death. No matter what point you are in your life, because He lives, His love yet remains. Where God's love remains, so does His grace and mercy.

God is gracious and merciful! Sometimes we use these words together and sometimes interchangeably. However, they are different. Grace is God's unmerited favor. Which means that nothing we do can earn this type of favor. It is a favor simply because He loves us. Mercy! Mercy is exercised through compassion. Mercy is being lenient towards a person when they deserve a harsher punishment. Grace and mercy may not be the same; however, they accompany one another. Think about it. God loves you and He's gracious, therefore, He doesn't punish you, not as your sins deserve; that is God being merciful!

In the latter part of Nehemiah 9:17 (KJV) it reads, " . . . but thou art a God ready to pardon, gracious and merciful, slow to anger, and of great kindness, and forsookest them not." Because of who God is, when He should have walked away from us, He showed us grace and mercy! When God had a chance to wipe us off the face of this earth, He remembered how much He loved us. That is some kind of love.

God is faithful. Faithful is being consistent, constant, dependable, unwavering! If God is all of those things, He cannot contradict Himself. Therefore, God is consistent in who He is. Now we can understand why we cannot equate God with man. It is in man's nature to change. Man is a soul living inside a terrestrial body. This body can form habits and attitudes, and man can become fickle. God is fixed! Numbers 23:19 (KJV) "God is not a man, that he should lie; neither the son of man, that he should repent: hath he not said it, and shall he not do it? or hath he spoken, and shall he not make it good?" Since God is faithful, we can trust Him with everything!

God is loving! Not only is God loving, but also, He is love. Remember when I mentioned that love is not carnal, it's spiritual. God is a spirit and He works in the spirit. God's love for us supersedes anything we could ever want. Our thing as single people is we want to feel goose bumps. We don't see how a spirit can give us butterflies. We can't comprehend how a spirit can leave us in awe, daydreaming, or love struck!

We have to step out of carnality to understand what it means when God stated in Jeremiah 31:3 (KJV) "… Yea, I have loved thee with an everlasting love…" This kind of love is a love that doesn't lose its intensity. This love cannot be extinguished. This love, whether reciprocated or not, is unconditional.

As a matter of fact, when our carnal mind expected God to fall out of love with us, He showed His greatest expression of His love. In Romans 5:6 (KJV) "For when we were yet without strength, in due time Christ died for the ungodly." Verse 8 "But God commendeth his love toward us, in that, while we were yet sinners, Christ died for us."

While we've blamed God for other's mistakes, He sent His son Jesus to die for us! While we were addicted, conflicted and afflicted as results to our various circumstances, Christ knew we would still try to hide it from Him and yet, He died for us! That is some kind of love; a love we can't comprehend.

We owe God a fighting chance. Not that God would lose a battle for our hearts. God is who He is, and God has His ways. However, it's the sacrifice and the willingness to yield to Him with a complete and total yes. God shouldn't have to wait for us to determine whether we want Him. We should be running to the safety of His arms.

Who wouldn't want to have a real encounter with God? He has loved you long before you existed. A God who loved you even when you were simply His thoughts!

What is God ultimately saying about this real encounter? Everything that we have been expecting to receive within a future or previous marriage starts with Him, our King! God desires for us to know Him intimately. This is not a sexual intimacy, which the connotation associated with intimately would normally suggest.

To know God intimately, to have a real encounter with God simply means that the encounter is personal and thorough. If we've been hiding ourselves from God because of fear, we are missing out on something spectacular.

God can give you goose bumps! He can leave you in awe and desiring more, but are you willing to open yourself up to that? Are you willing to let go of the notion that God is 'them?' 'Them,' are those who have hurt you. Are you willing to stop being the victim long enough to be a victor?

You don't have to forget those things that you've been carrying and attempt to hide them in order to have a real encounter with God. You have to be bold enough to say, "God, I'm the definition of imperfect. I got all this stuff, this emotional baggage, and I want to hide it. I want to hide it because it hurts. I want to hide it because I fear that if I expose myself to you, you'll see my nakedness as horrific. God, I fear that if I expose who I am to you, and all the ugly parts of my life, that you too will reject me like 'they did.' God, I fear that if I let go, I'll lose control. Control is the only thing I know. God, this is a struggle for me, but God, I trust you! I trust that you will see my wounds and you won't make them deeper, but that you will be my healer. God, I trust that if I let go, you will embrace me with a love that I need and desire."

We cannot allow fear to hinder us from embracing God. We'll never live life to the fullest potential if we live in fear. It's always going to be easier said than done. However, if you take the first step, each step after will be easier. For your every one step, God will take three. One step for Himself as the Father, one for Jesus, and one for the Holy Ghost!

The first step in a real encounter with God is letting go. I know it hurts. However, in order for the wounds to heal under your self-made bandages, it has to be exposed to some air. Being transparent again, I thought I had accomplished this with God. I thought I had exposed all my ugliness, but God kept bringing to the surface what I had buried deep. After it began to surface it was all the more hard to entreat God. I felt as though God, the creator of the entire universe should have rejected me. I rejected me! My sins were ugly and dark. I didn't grow up in church, so my track record started early. At a young age, and I do mean young (elementary school), I was dealing with some abominable stuff. I look back now and I see how God didn't allow the worst of the worst to ensnare me. However, He has called me despite of it all. I'll never understand why God chose me, called me, and why He yet loves me. That will always be a mystery. However, because He loves me enough to have called me out of darkness, I want to remain forever in His light. So --I had to let go.

I've had to cry, "God, this is the ugly part of me. God, if this part of me were revealed it'll be a life changer." God is a life changer. Once we let go, God can do a great thing in us.

Having a real encounter with God is seeking God for God. We don't seek God's face for the fish and the loaves. We don't seek God's face for the bonuses. God is not our sugar daddy! God is our father, and as a father, He naturally is a provider. You don't love your parents so they'll pay your rent and your car-note. You wouldn't want anyone to do that to you. This is another reason we can't have a real encounter with God; we have ulterior motives.

Matthew 6:33 (KJV) "But seek ye first the kingdom of God, and his righteousness; and all these things shall be added unto you." To paraphrase a commentary I was reading, if you seek out the spiritual things first, God will take care of the material things. Having a real encounter with God requires us to seek those things that are spiritual. WE need to be about our fathers' business first. Jesus taught us that.

To truly have an encounter with the King, our relationship with God has to mean more to us than anything. This will require us to set time apart every day to develop a relationship with Him. WE have to sacrifice. That means time dedicated to God and Him alone. The beautiful thing about being single is that we have the freedom to do this without having to be considerate of a spouse.

Right now, you can be selfish and do you and God, but when you're married, a consecration is an intricately planned event. You can't on a whim, go on a consecration where you are abstaining from intimacy with your husband, to be intimate with God without consulting your husband. I know we desire marriage, but take advantage of the fact that the only person you have to answer to is God! I wish we could visit that more now, but that is a different discussion.

An encounter with the King requires sacrifice and consecration. At some point, to go to a deeper depth in God, your Thursday night television programming is going to have to wait a week or two. To experience God in a capacity in which you never imagined, you are going to have to push back your plate for days at a time.

Have you ever wondered what it meant to go beyond the veil? In Exodus 26, it describes how the veil of the tabernacle divided the holy place and the most holy place. As a priest, Aaron and those from his lineage were permitted to enter into the holy place daily, but into the most holy or the holies of holies was to be entered into only once a year for atonement. To minister in that magnitude was not something to take lightly. Ill preparation would result in immediate death.

When Jesus yielded up the ghost, the veil of the temple was torn in two. It was ripped from the top to the bottom. The place where God once resided and could only be accessed by a high priest is now accessible to all who accepts Jesus. Jesus gave Himself as a perpetual sacrifice to redeem us back to God. Now, according to Hebrews 10: 27, we have the ability through our boldness to enter into the presence of God by the blood of Jesus. We can now go beyond the veil without seeing death. We are covered in the blood of Jesus. When we enter into the presence of God, God sees us through the blood of His son.

I'm glad I can go to God for myself. I'm glad that I can daily press my way into His presence. I'm glad that He has allowed me access. No matter how broken my life, I can entreat the King.

This chapter "An Encounter With the King," has significant meaning. As single women, we think that being single means God, the King has forgotten about us. The truth is, God has favored us more than we could have imagined.

Being married limits us in ways we'll never understand until we're married. In this season of our lives, God has given us an all access pass to Him! If you are familiar with the book of Esther, being single in this season of your life is as God holding out the golden scepter. What does that mean? You have obtained favor in God's sight. Now is a time like no other to seek the face of God. Aside from marriage, what you do you want from God?

James 4:8a (KJV) "Draw nigh to God, and he will draw nigh to you." Get close to the King, and the King will get closer to you.

An encounter by Webster's definition includes the meeting of something unexpected. The truth is, the fact that we can go and entreat the King of Kings is unexpected. However, the experience of being in His presence, that is personal and should be deliberate. No one can tell you what to expect in the presence of God. You have to find out for yourself. This means you must want God for yourself.

This is an individual walk. You have to know God for yourself. God wants us as single women to be married to Him first! This is the meat and potatoes of this chapter. We are the bride (the church, in which you are a part) of Christ, and God wants to be our first love!

This is going to lead us into the remainder of the book.

Every part of our relationship with God is preparing us for marriage. Think of your relationship with God as a dry run. However, your dry run never results in divorce. This is the only time you can be polyandrous, married to God and eventually to a man.

We have to be appealing to God first. It is in the 'potter's hand,' that God can make us into something that seems good for Him to make.

Being in the hands of God is an intimate encounter. It is in His hands and in His presence, that He will take the marred vessel and make it beautiful and whole again. Through this reconfiguration, God is using life and its various occurrences to prepare us to be incredible, anointed, effective, confident, compassionate, and balanced women.

When we make God our first love, and truly begin to allow Him to pull off the layers of debris from our lives, our highest goal in life will be to please Him. God has given so much to show His love, and what we give in return is not just our love, but also our appreciation. With every fiber of our being, we ought to love God. Matthew 22 verse 37 reads, " Jesus said unto him, Thou shalt love the Lord thy God with all thy heart, and with all thy soul, and with all thy mind." Verse 38, "This is the first and great commandment."

Intimacy with God, being in the potter's hands, brings true fulfillment. In order to know true joy, love, passion, and comfort, we need to take the time to know God. We are to yield ourselves over to being the apple of God's eye.

Embracing God's love and learning to love Him just for being God, will inevitably teach us how to love others, and eventually how to love our husbands.

We discussed earlier in this chapter how God is faithful. So often we look to men to be Mr. Perfect, which we'll talk about later, however, when we enter into a real relationship with God first, we will stop being so easily disappointed with the inconsistency of others. We'll learn that God is the only one who keeps all of His promises.

An encounter with the King, just like any other relationship, is not microwaveable. Being in the potter's hand, building an intimate relationship is going to take time and effort. Even those who have fallen in love at first sight had to put in some work!

These first two chapters were a foundation. They introduce two fundamental things that we Christian women need to be engaging in before we get engaged; a relationship with God, and ministry.

How can we desire God's best when we don't know what His best is? If we hide all our idiosyncrasies, our shortcomings, our hurting and dark places from God, we hide ourselves, and we'll never avail ourselves to receiving the best of God.

We can never have a true encounter unless we yield to the hands of the potter. In the intimacy of His hands, God will not only prepare us for Himself as a bride fit for her groom, but He will also prepare us for ministry and for marriage.

I pray that you begin to acknowledge that there are some things you've told God, 'hands off,' and that you allow Him to do the work in you that He desires. I pray that you begin to press into the presence of God, even with all the parts of you that you feel are ugly and horrific, and begin to allow God to peel off the scabs and dress your wounds with His love. I declare that every woman reading this book who has been receptive to your love, God will have a supernatural experience with you like never before. I pray heavenly father that they go beyond the veil and they bask in your presence and find the fulfillment that they need. Help us to build on this foundation, that we may position ourselves for the bonuses of being in love with you! In Jesus name, Amen!

Chapter

3

What's on the Menu?

———◦◦✦◦◦———

"W hat's on the Menu?" What an interesting title. When God gave me this title I thought, "innovative." It tickled me! Honestly. I love how creative God is, especially in how He imparts information. In the Bible, Jesus used parables to communicate the mysteries of the kingdom of God. He has now given us, "What's on the Menu?"

Up to this point, we haven't even addressed the title, and for good reasons. You don't build a house without laying a foundation on a lot that has been leveled and prepared. Likewise with those seeking to be married; you cannot talk your cute self into a marriage without being adequately prepared, especially if you are expecting God's best.

So, what's on the menu? Beautiful women of God, you are what's on the menu. This is in no means objectifying you, or an attempt to make you feel degraded or debased. Society has already done enough of that.

Have you ever had a taste for something, but you couldn't quite pinpoint what it was? In order to figure it out, you went to a restaurant you knew served food that you liked. It wasn't until you looked at the menu, that your taste buds and your eyes came into a perfect harmony on what would satiate you.

This is why, for an analogy (parable) to explore the mystery of marriage, you are the menu. Mr. Right, which we will address in the next chapter, is looking for someone to satiate or fulfill his desires for marriage. Mr. Right knows only one place where he can go, sit down, look at the menu, and find what he is looking for, God! God is the owner of the restaurant, and the restaurant, the Holy Ghost.

The best part about Mr. Right coming to view the menu is that he can order anything he wants and it wouldn't be considered gluttonous. God has specially crafted everything on the menu for Mr. Right! That's right, everything on the Menu was put there because God knew what he would come looking for. Amazing!

Owners handcraft their menus to be appealing to a specific audience. To ensure what they offer on the menu is appealing and of great quality, owners sample everything on the menu. They use nothing but the best ingredients. They want nothing but the best to be served because they want to cater to consumers of nothing but the best. They are of course expecting nothing short of great success.

God is continuously handcrafting you as a menu to be appealing to an audience of one, Mr. Right! God is not lazy, cheap, insouciant, or good at cutting corners. God is deliberate, meticulous, and extravagant. God works out things in His divine timing. He is using nothing but the best of Himself to prepare you, the menu, for the one man He's had in mind for you since before you two were born!

This is the best and only love triangle you should ever want to be in. Before we address that, let's continue to unveil why as an analogy, you are the menu.

As the menu, you first must appeal to the owner, God. The first two chapters built the foundation for the entire book. We are God's before He gives us away in marriage. Not only is God preparing us for Himself, but God also is simultaneously preparing us for Mr. Right.

As the owner, God is knowledgeable about what His target audience is searching for. God Himself has a particular palate that can only be satiated with what you have to offer. It is amazing how what God wants is what the target audience is looking for.

How is that possible? There are a few things God brought to my attention regarding this. As a Christian woman and a child of God, understand that it is not God's desire to have you unevenly yoked with a man who doesn't share the same beliefs, values, and standards as you do. Unless God specifically sends you on an evangelistic mission such as Hosea, please know the former is true. This is why Mr. Right himself will be so engulfed and wrapped up with his own relationship with the Father, that your intimate relationship with God becomes attractive to him.

However, it's not just your intimate relationship with God that will have him stoked. Once you have experienced God's love, nothing will ever fair in comparison. When Mr. Right recognizes the love of God dwelling in you, he'll be able to relate because it dwells in him.

As a menu, it is a requirement that you have something to offer. If you, as a woman were to take the time and effort to go to your favorite restaurant, sit down, and spend ten minutes or more searching for something that you know they serve, only to find out that for the time being they now only serve chips, salsa and water, you'd be highly disappointed. Why give you a menu, right?

For you to only be appealing to an audience of one, Mr. Right would be disappointed, disgusted and discouraged if he came to God looking for you, to only find out that God told him you never were open to taste testing and proper preparation. So unfortunately, you have nothing within yourself that will satisfy his desires in marriage. Technically, as his wife, you would have been the one woman who could fulfill all his desires in marriage. Therefore, God offers him water to go along with his chips and salsa due to your lack of preparation.

What does the water along with chips and salsa represent? Water is needed by every living organism to survive. Our bodies are composed of sixty percent of water. Every biological reaction that takes place within our bodies requires water or produces water as a byproduct.

Metaphorically speaking, family is like water to Mr. Right. God will surround him with family to quench his desire to start his own. God will allow his family to be more available and discerning to his needs. One can become full off of water, but that is a temporary fix. Water is tasteless; it is not meant to satiate permanently. It does not appease the deep longing for what's on the menu, regardless of it being needed to survive.

Chips and salsa anyone? I'm laughing hysterically. I love chips and salsa, but for me, I can't have chips and salsa without wanting guacamole. Having all three makes me crave Mexican food. I like steak. So having carne asada tacos one day makes me crave steak and shrimp another day, which leads me down a spiral of cause and effect.

Chips and salsa are like Mr. Right's friends. People who are encouraging, supportive, praying, loving and inspiring, will surround Mr. Right. But they are surrounding him with their husbands and wives. Eventually, he realizes that these relationships intensify his cravings for his own family! He didn't go to God looking for chips and salsa! That is not what he has a taste for. He's going to be left desiring more because he wants what's on the menu!

Whoever your Mr. Right may be, will weary God until God is able to produce what is on the menu. It's not that God can't, it's simply that we haven't. Wow! It happens all the time.

You've been in church where a woman fresh out of sin gets saved and is growing in the Lord. She is active in ministry. You think she's trying to start a church of her own, when in actuality, she is on fire for God! Sooner than you think, her marriage is being announced to a minster that has been attending the church for years. You are dumbstruck and wondering when God forgot about you.

He hasn't. God has been wearying you to get it right, because Mr. Right has been wearying Him. Forget Mr. Right wearying God; you weary God and God wearies you in return to get yourself together. You don't believe me and I know you don't because as I stated, I am where you are. However, God through the writing of this book has removed the veil from my eyes.

God will tell us to fast until three for a week, and we fast two days until noon. During that taste test, it's revealed that was a bad batch of obedience. God tells us to go pray for that sister who we heard was talking about us behind our backs. What do we do? We come up with every excuse why we shouldn't go pray for her. That was a bad batch of forgiveness. God tells us to cut all communication with the man who we know doesn't have the same standards we have. What happens? Maybe we backslide, and maybe we get our heart broken. That's a bad batch of trust. We didn't trust the direction and leading of God. We didn't trust that our God knows what He's doing.

So then, because of all the bad batches during God's taste test, God has to result in giving Mr. Right water to go with his chips and salsa. Simply put, we have nothing to offer if we do not prepare.

Do you see why a relationship with the King is so important first? God doesn't want to bless you to be in a good marriage where you two were created specifically for each other only to find out you didn't complete the preparation. If you went to a restaurant and the food was undercooked, you would have a fit. Beyond that, it would make you sick. Something that was meant to bring nourishment to you, if it wasn't prepared properly would make you sick and disappointed. Likewise with seeking marriage, you don't want to have a good man, and I do mean a good man, and because you weren't adequately prepared, instead of bringing him nourishment and fulfillment, you make him sick!

Let's be real; most of us women who are looking to be married do not want a man who doesn't have it together. As a matter of fact, some of us have a list. We'll talk about that more when we challenge the title, "Mr. Right." However, if a man doesn't come close to what we have on our list, we dismiss him. Funny. How do you know Mr. Right hasn't been checking you out, but because you are not prepared, he keeps dismissing you, sending back the menu over and over again because it has nothing to offer him? Reread that! This is a continuous dismissal because you were created for an audience of one.

Small disclaimer, yes, some men and women will marry people who they love tremendously, outside of the divine will of God. I believe that if the right man or woman is unavailable due to a lack of preparation, God's permissive will is enacted and the marriage can be successful. However, there will always be some form of lack if it's not the right man or woman. A woman can offer something similar to the real thing, but the servings are too small and the price a little bit more costly. In the end, Mr. Right will only get a fraction of what he needs, and he settles never knowing what it feels like to be satiated. The reverse is true too. It goes without saying, I want God's divine will for my life.

The reason that Mr. Right will weary God until you're ready, and I'm crazy enough to believe it since God created one man and one woman to join together in holy matrimony, is because he senses your proximity. Before God reveals you to each other, you both will mutually attract (exert a drawing force on) the other.

Were we not drawn to God and didn't even know why? Did not His love captivate us before we understood it? We'll never be able to fully comprehend God's love toward us, however, one day we found ourselves in a position, a condition which led us to the altar to stop what we were doing and kneel and repent. Eventually, this led to salvation. He drew you!

Your relationship with God prepares you for marriage, and once you have positioned yourselves in God, God will allow you and Mr. Right to mutually draw each other. Mr. Right may be drawing you because he is in position and ready, but you may not be drawing him because of your lack of preparation.

God has a great plan for your life. However, it was all meant to start with Him. He never intended for us to get so consumed in a desire that it dominates our thought process or hinders how we function. Let God prepare you as a menu, to be a place of fulfillment for that right man.

Chapter

4

Mr. Right Out the Door

———————

D id you read the title of this chapter? Of course you did, but did you really read it. Like -did you take a moment to consider what was meant by, "Mr. Right Out the Door?"

It has multiple meanings. First things first, "Mr. Right," is a heavy title that we are trying to put on lightweights. Secretly when we are saying that we are looking and waiting for Mr. Right, we truly are expecting Mr. Perfect.

Before you disagree with me, let's explore this a tad bit further.

Mr. Right has no real substance because it is vague. What is he right for? Fixing the sink, cooking, paying bills? Let's be honest, the one reason we all have these grocery lists of what comprises a Mr. Right, is because he has to meet certain expectations. So, this title becomes loaded with expectations, which is why in today's society Mr. Right = Mr. Perfect. Ladies, we all know that there is no such thing as Mr. Perfect.

Why else is Mr. Right such a loaded title? The definition of right means, the best or the most suitable of a number of possible choices for a particular purpose or occasion. You might be thinking 'exactly,' Mr. Right is the best choice out of all the possible choices I have to join together in holy matrimony.

Wrong! Do you know the limits we put on God and His divine will when we assume that there is more than one man for us to choose from?

To have fewer options seems like a limitation; it is that same mentality that causes some people to go through marriages like mints. We are looking at multiple candidates, but God created one! Again, we've forgotten the first marriage. Eve had no choice in being Adam's wife. God presented Eve to Adam. Adam was asleep when God made Eve. Adam didn't put in a special order about her bust, hips, or looks! God saw his desire! We'll dig into this a little deeper further on down the heavenly brick road.

What I am saying is; you can create your grocery list on how he should look, talk, smell, dress and conduct himself all you want, but the truth is, God has already considered who you are and knows what you stand in need of. That is from your most basic needs even to the complexity of whom you will marry. Therefore, women, I am so sorry to rain on your parade, but Mr. Right doesn't exist.

Mr. Right, is also very rigid. Meaning the title has no flexibility. He has to be so perfect, that he can't fail at living up to your conditions. Once Mr. Right makes a mistake and falls short, and he will, we're ready to kick him to the curb. We assume, because he didn't work, that 'he's not the one God has for me.' How would you know? While you've concocted how tall he has to be, his complexion, his eye color, his shoe size, and breadth of his chest, you've arrested the divine hand of God. The man God has for you may be two shades darker or three shades lighter than you would like, but nevertheless, he's the only man God knows can give you the companionship you've been praying for. While we are Christians, we are still women, so don't pretend you haven't at some point at least hinted to God what Mr. Right ought to look like.

This is why Mr. Right = Mr. Perfect. Can you uphold your own list and be 'Mrs. Perfect?' Let's completely flip the script. How is your credit? Do you make the kind of money you are expecting him to make? No, you just want somebody to pamper you 24 hours of the day, right? That's unrealistic. He cannot pamper you 365 days a year if you're expecting him to bring home six figures a year! Mr. Right is rigid. To make six figures a year means your husband will be spending a lot more time at work than he does at home. Think about this, what kind of hours does an emergency room doctor work?

If the script was truly flipped, how is your Honda Civic running in comparison to the approximately $230,000 dollar Mercedes S 65 AMG

Coupe you are expecting Mr. Right to drive? We need to be able to meet our own list of must-haves!

I know God gets His shares of laughs, because not only do we write the list, we pray diligently about these lists. 'God, please let him be supportive, understanding, loving, gentle, kind, honest, generous, forgiving, and God, don't forget handsome.' I know the list goes on. Some of us load so many details in these lists, 'God, don't let one toe-nail be darker than the other,' that we begin to write in the margins and in very small print; both front and back!

Are we truly expecting God to drop a robot out of the heavens? That is what you are asking God for when you make your grocery list. Mr. Right and Mr. Perfect, those are shallow, superficial, inflated and false titles for both men and women. There is nothing wrong with desiring certain qualities in a husband, but realize that God is not your special order cook.

When I say it's okay to desire certain characteristics from a man, I'm being serious. But when I say, God is not your special order cook, that means, when you say you want a supportive husband, don't demand our God and King to make your husband supportive in everything. That's usually what we're saying. There may be times when you do things outside of the will or directives of God, and as the head of his house, your husband will respectfully disagree and not show his support. That doesn't make him any less your husband or less supportive. That makes him wise.

Realize that no man is perfect. If you expect a man to be perfect, you'll never accept that he will make mistakes. We all do! Some of us have Mr. Right on such a high pedestal, that if God were to bless us right now, we'd blaspheme God the second Mr. Right disappointed us. That is not healthy. I've gleaned enough from married folk to know that your spouse, no matter how in love you two are, they will occasionally irritate you.

Mr. Right is not a god, so trust and believe he will irritate you at some point in time. Simply because you are emotionally driven and most men are not, that will frustrate you. The fact that he can't relate to every situation as you do, that will frustrate you. Most men don't have much to say when they've exhausted most of their patience during the day, and trust me, that will frustrate you. Mr. Perfect, also known as Mr. Right, DOES NOT EXIST! I'm not yelling, wink, wink… I'm just saying.

Now, here is where we get distinguished. There may not be a Mr. Right

29

or Mr. Perfect, however, there is a Mr. Right-for-you. For every one man there is one right woman, and vice versa. Imagine a jigsaw puzzle with only five pieces. In the puzzle, you have The Father, The Son and the Holy Ghost, and two other pieces that fit perfectly together. Neither of those two pieces are perfect! They are slightly flawed for whatever reason; however, those two pieces are perfect together and help to establish the big picture.

Together, a husband and a wife, both imperfect, function together to help manifest and unearth the divine will of God. Each of the two is a working part which is made more powerful, influential, convincing and resilient together!

Oh! It makes sense doesn't it? This is why it is so important to have your own personal and intimate relationship with the King! I'll reiterate that as many times as God tells me to, because this is key.

It is our relationship with God that will bring us to a place where we can be joined to another, and where we can obtain a greater capacity for ministry. It is very unlikely that your grocery list included you marrying Mr. Right-for-you so that you would have a greater capacity for ministry. 'Lord, let the husband you bless me with allow me to have a greater capacity for ministry. Heavenly father, that would be the icing on the cake.' Uh… no. Be real with yourself, because you know that wasn't in your prayer.

We don't think about marriage itself as a ministry. We don't understand its function so we pray superficially. As a matter of fact, we don't know what we ought to be praying for to begin with. This is the first reason we are throwing, Mr. Right, out the door.

To further expound on a previous thought, let us look at Romans 8:26-27 (KJV). Verse 26, "Likewise the Spirit also helpeth our infirmities: for we know not what we should pray for as we ought: but the Spirit itself maketh intercession for us with groaning's which cannot be uttered." Verse 27, "And he that searcheth the hearts knoweth what is the mind of the Spirit, because he make intercession for the saints according to the will of God."

Say what? We don't even know what to pray for. While we are praying in the spirit, it is the Holy Ghost that will intercede on our behalf! Amazing. The Holy Ghost isn't just making intercession for our spiritual well-being, He is interceding on our behalf --period.

We think we know what we want, but only God knows what we want and really need. The Holy Ghost confers with God on our behalf on a constant basis. Why are we making these lists? Did we consult with the Holy Ghost while making these lists?

There are things in our lives that we almost did, but had the Holy Ghost not directed us in a different direction, we would have gone astray.

If the Holy Ghost can interpret my groaning's which I can't through the English language articulate, why wouldn't I want to seek God about what I desire? The great thing is, God is already in touch with our desires. We just have to yield them over to Him.

There is nothing wrong with having standards. Going back to the analogy of a Menu, every restaurant has to uphold certain safety standards. The menu does not create the standards; it embodies the standards. However, don't have standards and secretly hope that a man will challenge them.

This chapter is meant to expose the shallowness of the title Mr. Right, and to help us all get on the same page. He doesn't exist. However, there is a Mr. Right-for-me! Which means he isn't perfect, but he is perfect for me.

The real question then becomes; do you trust God? In His infinite wisdom, immaculate creativity, and unquenchable love for you, has God ever made a mistake? Only He knows the frailty of our hearts, intricacy of our minds, our deepest desires and our every need.

Do you trust God? If you do, why can't you trust Him with your heart? Oh, you do? You sincerely trust the heart of the father? When it comes to marriage, God is like a father who is anxious about giving away His daughter in marriage. Any real father would tell you that they don't just want anybody to have their daughter.

God is worse. You are not just God's child, but you are His investment. Guess what? He wants a return. Therefore, while He was creating you, God considered your personality, your idiosyncrasies, your pet peeves, your short and long-term goals, your shortcomings, and everything else that matters or affects you. God has one man in mind that can handle all of you; a man who will not be intimidated by you.

You have a preference for a certain kind of man and God knows that. He also understands how that particular palate developed. Hmm? Developed? Yes, God knows how the desire to have a muscular built, tall, and attractive husband developed. Some of our desires were not birthed positively, or from chaste places. It's not because we've seen how a muscular, tall and attractive husband operated in a good marriage. That description is either from what you have experienced in previous relationships, or a fantasy created by television.

Some of us have developed preconceived notions of what a certain man is 'like'. Like being, what he is like sexually. Oh yes, I went there because it's true. Tying this back into chapter two, we can never be delivered fully if we are not honest with ourselves and with God.

Some of us reading this book are not virgins. We haven't always been saved and guess what? There is no condemnation in Christ; therefore, the only person holding it over your head is the adversary, the devil.

Please understand, however, that Mr. Right-for-you, may not be one to throw you against a wall every night in the heat of the moment. That may be something you liked with a man you were with before you knew Christ or after you backslid. God wants us to be whole. Preconceived notions have got to go. Which means we have to get rid of some things we didn't even consider to be an issue.

You know why you like a certain type of man, but it may not be healthy. Entering into a divinely established marriage where this man was meant for you and only you, and you expect him to not only be perfect, but match a previous lover in how you two consummate your marriage, will cause Mr. Right-for-you to walk right out the door.

Oh yes! Right out the door he will go. This leads us back to, do we trust God? Do we trust that he will take care of us even in marriage?

I like listening to women who are recently married or have been married for a while and they are shocked at how great their husbands are. It's not that when they were courting that he wasn't a great man, but she didn't enter marriage with false expectations. She accepted him for who he was, and not what she expected him to be. Who he is, as a matter of fact, exceeds what she could have ever asked for, but she left all expectations in the hands of God.

Realize that God is well acquainted with you. However, God cannot bless you with Mr. Right-for-you if you don't first throw out the fact that he will not be perfect. Accept that you both will make mistakes. You also need to get rid of all preconceived notions that you brought from other relationships whether they are positive or negative. Understand that God works best with a blank canvas.

It is my hope and prayer that this chapter has enlightened you.

Dear heavenly father, we thank you for the journey you are taking us on. This journey will bring us closer to you. God, teach us to trust you with everything that concerns us; our heart, mind, and our soul. Thank you for considering all our desires well before you established this earth. Help us to grasp that you know everything we truly stand in need of. God, we yield to you the blank canvas of our desires and we know that you will create something spectacular. Teach us to lean and depend on you for everything. Everything we've tried to hold onto from previous relationships, we first ask that you forgive us. Help us to let go completely, that we may be whole lacking nothing. In Jesus name, Amen!

Chapter 5

The Blessing in One

———————

Before we delve a little deeper into the significance of the menu, Mr. Right-for-you, the owner, the restaurant, and chips and salsa, we first must recognize something very powerful and seemingly problematic; the blessing in one.

This seems unorthodox since there are so many men in the world to choose from. However, we have the wrong perspective.

To begin, I'll give my personal testimony that will help establish the substratum of this chapter.

While in college, I was in a relationship for a little over two years. In this relationship I never felt appreciated or good enough. It wasn't that he, the young man I was dating, wasn't appreciative, or that he never showed gratitude. The reason I never felt good enough is not because he was so great and I was insignificant.

To be honest, I've come to realize the reason I felt the way that I did is because I was naïve. For starters, I tried to give him everything I would give to my husband. I attempted to show him what life would be like if we were married while we were dating.

I showered him with my love, attention, support, and comfort. I cooked for him, and I only cook for people that I care tremendously for, especially with all that I had going on. Although the very existence of our relationship was sinful, I prayed for him when I wasn't so caught up in what I thought we had going on.

What did we have going on? Honestly, there was no fruit to show for all the effort and attention that I was investing into this relationship. I was carrying a burden that I didn't have to. I was giving of myself in ways I didn't have to. Why? Because I thought I was in love. I figured if I loved him, he would eventually love me in return and the way I deserved. That resulted in me tolerating disappointment after disappointment. I dealt with lies upon lies, and an unfaithful lover. After I had finally gotten sick in my mess, God opened my eyes. I was never created to have to endure that. In that relationship, the young man didn't have the capacity for what I had to offer. Therefore, I was always forcing it to work, and while doing so, I carried the load alone.

Going back for a moment, he didn't have the capacity. There is that word capacity again. He couldn't be receptive of all that I gave because he didn't have the ability or power to experience and comprehend the love I was showing because it was not meant for him. This is why I say I was naïve; there was a lack of understanding and wisdom on my part.

Capacity shows both what you can hold to keep, or reserve as in storage, and what you are able to give in return. Therefore, it was not that this young man was never gracious and appreciative of what I was attempting to do, but his gratitude matched his capacitance. Due to my ignorance at the time, I felt I was inadequate in my attempts to show genuine love, therefore, I never felt good enough at loving him. Instead of stopping in my tracks, I tried harder. This was a result of never receiving adequate returns and desperately wanting one.

What I felt was my downfall, loving hard, is actually a blessing. I gave what should have been for my husband to someone who in fact was never created to be Mr. Right-for me! However, with the current revelation from my past situation, I've come to realize that my future husband will have a far greater capacity for what I have to offer, and he will feel like the king of the world.

I endured hurt because of my ignorance. It was birthed from the desire to have what I invested into a relationship bring me a return. But God! When God created me, He gave me a natural emotional spring called, resilience! I've bounced back. I've become a better woman knowing that

1. I do have something to offer and 2. God created only one man who can handle all of me, and that's because there is blessing in one.

While that scar was difficult to share, because who knows, out of curiosity, my future husband may have picked up this book, it was necessary. I realize the tool this is to help glean in God's field.

Too often we get lonely while waiting for God to move on our behalf. We watch our friends get married, have children, pursue careers and we feel stuck. So we jump into relationship after relationship hoping and praying that God has sent one of these men into our lives to fulfill the purpose of becoming our husbands. Realize and know that when you were being tempted to enter into the last relationship, Mr. Right-for-you was on his way. He walked through doors of the restaurant and sat down, but the menu was unavailable.

Ha! God is amazing. We feel waiting just a little while longer is waiting forever.

There is a blessing in one. Think of it this way. God created only one man in the world who could even begin to come close to loving you the way that God does. There is only one man, who can truly appreciate you for the woman that God designed you to be. There is only one man who will come to know your thought pattern better than your subconscious mind. God created only one man for you that gets you, and sees you. Not the superficial you that you show the world to avoid judgment. Your future husband will see beyond that. He'll see beyond the make-up, designer clothes, insecurities, faults, and see the piece of himself, his desire, that God used to create you into this woman he'd only dreamed of, that is until the day he saw you; or sees you! That's not a fairytale, that's real ya'll!

Excuse my sudden change in vernacular, however, we've grown so accustomed to the commonness of divorce, that we've forgotten that marriage is truly a beautiful thing. Ergo, we jump at the first opportunity at dating, getting engaged, or married without considering if this is whom God predestined for us to marry.

Divorce has become so acceptable in today's society that men and women alike are flying through marriages trying to find the right one. They've lost the conviction, appreciation, and respect for marriage. Please be reminded that Jesus said that He didn't come to do away with the law, He came to fulfill the law. That doesn't give us the right to disrespect something that God has deemed holy.

Besides, it only takes one! One husband and one wife, joined together to become one flesh. God gave us this equation since the beginning.

Let's look at Genesis 2: 22-24 (KJV) one verse at a time.

Verse 22 reads, "And the rib, which the lord God had taken from man, made he a woman, and brought her unto the man." From one man, God took a rib, to create a woman. This is singular. God did not create more than one woman and asked Adam which one he wanted. There are so many nuggets of wisdom in this one verse, but for now, we'll just focus on the one.

Verse 23, "And Adam said, This is now bone of my bones, and flesh of my flesh: she shall be called Woman, because she was taken out of Man." The big thing we will consider here are the words "of my." Remember that the word of relates a part to a whole. The way that this is structured shows the uniqueness of Eve. God could have formed Eve from the dust of the ground and breathed into her nostrils the breath of life. Instead, God took from the man to form the woman. He took a piece of Adam to form a depiction of his desires, Eve, and then rejoined her, Adam's desire manifested, back to Adam through marriage. Oh my God! This creates a distinct connection between a man and a woman who are to be joined together as husband and wife.

A wife fundamentally is a part of her husband. She was designed in the womb of her mother with her husband in mind. God had seen her husband's desire from the beginning of time and used that as He was fashioning her in the womb. This seems like a reach, but it's not. Read the verses over starting from verse eighteen.

God saw Adam's need before Adam ever noticed his lack. Adam had no idea of what a helpmeet for him would look like. He had no way of articulating his desire, but God understood the elaborateness of his heart. Therefore, He constructed woman from the very thing that desired her; bone of his bone, flesh of his flesh.

Metaphorically speaking, when you feel something way down in your bones, it has great significance. It represents a deep longing, spiritual if you will. However, when something gives you goose bumps, that is surface. Something that is surface appeals to the senses. Eve ultimately fulfills a range of desires, from the deep longing parts of Adam to the sensual parts of him. Which is why Adam is able to say she is bone of my bone and flesh of my flesh.

Verse 24 goes on to say, "Therefore shall a man leave his father and his mother, and shall cleave unto his wife: and they shall be one flesh." One man and one woman, two people, shall join together to form one flesh. That's it, that's all, there's no need to continue.

However, if you will, when we really realize the advantage of there being only one, we won't be so obsessed with which one he may be. We can take comfort in the arms of God knowing that He has the perfect one for us. If there is only one man for me, then I'll wait patiently in the arms of God, because anyone who isn't, is a waste of effort and time. That is very uncompromising. To be honest, I don't want to further compromise and risk never receiving what God has for me because I think I know better than God.

Another way of looking at this is to consider God's divine will and His permissive will. Which one do you prefer? Do you want what you want, or do you want what God has? I can guarantee what God has is much better than what you want.

God will allow some people to marry, divorce and remarry in sad cycles because all they wanted was what they wanted. They settled for what they figured was God's best for them. Love, that is God's permissive will. He will permit it to happen in order to teach us and help us mature. However, with God's divine will, oh my goodness, that's a blessing in itself. Since God's knows what's best for me, I'll trust that what He has for me is far greater than what I could imagine for myself.

When we really come to understand the blessing that there is in one, it will get easier to resist the decoys. Understand that everything walking like, talking like, and acting like the real thing, isn't. The more you draw closer to God, the more He will begin to reveal the tactics of the enemy.

In the beauty of God's divine timing, He will reveal you and your future husband to one another.

I've been told that when I talk about marriage that I sound as if I'm speaking of a fairytale. They are basically saying I have an unrealistic view of marriage. That saddens me for them, not for myself.

Why are fairytales fictional? It's definitely not because they have happy endings. It's the route by which the characters in the stories achieve their happy endings. Sure we as women are not pricking our fingers on needles, falling into a deep sleep and awaiting our true love's kiss. That is definitely fictional, but living happily ever after, that's all God!

This is what saddens me; some people have married without realizing that while there may be challenges within a marriage, that God in fact has created it to be blissful. Their thinking if you would, is inverted; 'I've entered into this marriage realizing that it may be blissful at times, but it was created to be full of challenges.' What? It sounds crazy, but when you marry someone God didn't predestine for you to marry, this will be your testimony. I'm not going to marry someone looking for bliss in seasons. I'll have bliss in my marriage year round, but challenges? Challenges will have designated seasons.

If you marry outside the will of God, I'm not saying you can't be happy. Consequently, like some people, what God ordained, will appear to you as a fairytale. What then happens, because only every good and perfect gift comes from God, is you take the risk of being in a marriage you actually don't want to be in. Not because you don't want to be married or that you don't love that person, but you see how marriage is supposed to flow and you realize that your marriage lacks such flow.

Without going on a complete tangent, what then arises is another issue that has become popular, adultery. Husbands and wives begin stepping outside of their marriages because they are unfulfilled by the ones they have. 'Side pieces,' if you will, are operating in the role by which a husband should be to his wife, or a wife to her husband. It only takes one, but know that it takes the right one!

We should take pride in knowing that not just any man can have us as his wife. It takes a certain kind of man to love you the way that you ought to be loved as a woman.

When you visit a real nice restaurant, they will bring the menu to you once you are seated. Once your future husband and you have both gotten into position, which we'll discuss later, God will bring you to him, in God's perfect timing.

As with most of the chapters, I don't want it to end without praying to God on your behalf. Father, I thank you for being God. You are omniscient, so you know everything. You are aware of every relationship we've entered, desperately hoping that it would result in marriage. You know the investments we've made and how God we've sought for returns. Help us to realize that there is only one man that you handcrafted to have the capacity to receive our love and return it with interest. Halt our searches, and help us to relax and be content in you, knowing that at the right moment, you will bring us to our Mr. Right-for-us! Thank you for being all that we truly need. In Jesus name, Amen!

Chapter

6

The Menu

———◦◦◦———

We have already established that each woman reading this book, is the menu. From this point on, we are going to work our way backwards; meaning we are going to explore you as a woman first, and continue our journey to the very God who created you. We'll explore you in creation naturally and according to the analogy created within this book.

A few major areas in which we'll go into detail for this chapter is, what do you really have to offer as a woman? This ultimately will lead to our next discussion of where God has you housed. Spiritually and naturally, where are you? The place where you are, are God's desires being fulfilled through you? And finally, what's in it for you?

A Fruit To Be Desired

———◦◦◦———

Society objectifying women has become vastly derogatory. In times past it was meant to help men understand our complexity. We are and will always be different than our male counterparts. How we view the world will always be different because we take a lot more into consideration than a man.

To look at a flower, a man will see that it is yellow. For a woman, sure we'll acknowledge that the color is yellow, however, we will also realize that it's not as vibrant because it's beginning to wilt. We consider its lack of water, or the fact that it has been in the sun constantly. We see beyond what sometimes is there because we were created this way.

As women, we tend to be more detail oriented, which is a part of our nature as being nurturing. We don't simply care for and encourage the maturation or success of our children and families, but ideas, visions and goals of people who surround us. Often times the ideas, visions and goals that we stimulate and cultivate are not always our own. We stimulate other people's minds; we help them brainstorm to expand their concepts and visions. We help foster and establish new relationships. This is why women have been objectified as gossipers. Unfortunately, whether you do or not, euphemistically speaking, this umbrella covers all women to some extent because of our social skills.

We are social beings. WE love to talk. Whether we talk about other people, ideas, whatever, or ourselves we women love to talk. Therefore, at times, we are both assets and liabilities. Interesting pitfall, we have been raised in a society where apparently there can only be one alpha female in a social group. At one point we're building someone up and the next we are tearing them down. What is disheartening is that this kind of attitude and thinking has crept its way into the church. This behavior on women of God has made us look like liabilities.

Christian women we are supposed to be a light to the women in the world. In 2 Corinthians chapter 6, Paul talks about not being unequally yoked with unbelievers. Verse 14, "Be ye not unequally yoked together with unbelievers; for what fellowship hath righteousness with unrighteousness? and what communion hath light with darkness?" There has to be a distinction between unbelieving women and believing women. As Christian women seeking to be married, we should epitomize being an asset than a liability.

If we are to offer anything to God and to our future husbands we need to be an asset rather than a liability. We cannot offer a Holy God a secular sacrifice. Our oblations and sacrifices have to be acceptable before God. What is considered acceptable? John 4: 24 (KJV) "God is a spirit; and they that worship him must worship him in spirit and in truth." Do not bring your carnal offerings to a Holy God. How do you worship in truth if you don't know who God is? Hebrews 11:4 (KJV) "But without faith it is impossible to please him: for he that cometh to God must believe that he is, and that he is a rewarder of them that diligently seek him." It is impossible to have faith in a God you know nothing about. That's right! It's all about a relationship with God. I don't want God to reject me because I've become a liability to Him.

God will not offer a preordained, perfect-for-us, godly and righteous husband a worldly woman. Remember that Mr. Right-for-you will have his own relationship with God. He desires God's best just as you do. He wants peace, love and happiness just as you do. Mr. Right-for-you wants to smile when he sees you coming. Men get butterflies too! As a liability attempting to be married before you have prepared yourself, you risk Mr. Right-for-you saying to God, 'I'd rather starve or survive on chips and salsa the rest of my life than take that risk.' Ouch!

Are you an inconvenience, risk or embarrassment; or are you a valuable investment that brings joy?

When you first accepted Christ as your Lord and Savior, the desire to know God and get closer to Him, allowed you the boldness to cut away things out of your life that no longer fit. Some friends had to go because of the influence they would have on your life. Certain ways of thinking and acting you changed. You stopped using colorful language because the Holy Spirit convicted you. You were being transformed into the image of Christ because your darkened life was being illuminated. You were being transformed from a liability to an asset.

God being God can use anyone He chooses, and as a liability, He could have still used you, but only limitedly. You'd never truly be able to give Him a full return on His investment unless you were an asset.

As a result of being an asset, with the unique and intricate way God created us to be as women, from our different idiosyncrasies, proclivities, and propensities we have something to offer. What we are supposed to be offering is considered precious and rare in today's society.

You ever wonder why in movies you always hear a mother telling her son he should go to church to find him a nice wife? As Christian women, we offer something different. Although, there is a remarkable decline in the differences between secular women and godly women, when you have a real relationship with God, there is a certain, je ne sais quoi, being interpreted, something you can't quite put your finger on, when it comes to godly women.

This is one of the things that will draw Mr.Right-for-you, to you. If you would, this is what gave God goose bumps when He simply thought of you. Now that you are a physical being in creation, God's thoughts haven't changed. However, are you an asset or a liability?

What do you have to offer? Do you meet the qualifications of being a blessing, a benefit, an advantage, or providing strength, fortitude and virtue first to God and then to your future husband? That is what an asset is and what she does.

This was vaguely considered earlier in the book, but here is where we expound. We talked about how God is in the business of taste testing. This is only established through your relationship with God.

When God is taste testing, what is He looking for? What pleases our God? Often times religion, not God, has given women the assignment of sitting down in silence and looking pretty, as though this is the only way we are to function as women. However, we serve a greater function.

Because we are women, which are loving, nurturing, detailed oriented, persistent, patient, and sometimes quite outspoken there is a great work that we can do to advance God's agenda. It takes Him refining us to get out of us what He wants. He has to make slight or dramatic changes here and there to ensure what we offer qualifies us as an asset.

So we go through taste tests. These taste tests are divinely orchestrated or divinely permitted devices used to determine whether we possess the fruit of the spirit amongst other qualifying characteristics and mannerisms. Let's walk through them.

Do you have love to offer? Are you willing and able to give of yourself, sometimes sacrificially, with pure intentions, without considering if it would be returned? That is the core of what it means to love. Often times we are looking to be married in order to be loved. We are looking at marriage as a means to receive and not to give. As with our personal walks with God, we are looking to get something out of it, instead of considering what we can offer.

If you are reading this book it means you woke up this morning. If you woke up this morning you are still living under God's grace and His mercy! If you are still living under God's grace and mercy you have experienced His unconditional love. God has given freely of Himself to you every day of your life, without conditions. That means there are no stipulations to be a recipient of His love. His hope, however, is that you return the love, by dedicating your life to Him. He will always love you whether you love Him or not. The benefits, thus comes with the dedication of your life through relationship.

Once you have built a solid relationship with God, your intentions to seek God for material gain will become non-existent. All your intentions will eventually have changed when you know God for yourself.

Your objectives to one day marry for love will have changed. Your ambition will no longer be to get married, to find a husband who loves you, recipient; but to find someone who you can intimately share the love of God with, giver. Disclaimer, there is nothing wrong with desiring to be loved in a marriage. That is natural. However, we shouldn't seek marriage as a means only to receive.

This is a strange concept in today's society. I've had people tell me, that I should marry a man who loves me more than I love him. I've also come to realize that a majority of these women highlight their husband's inadequacies and therefore, never have an opportunity to enjoy their husbands for the men that they are. These women easily take their husband's love and affection for granted, and also will never be able to embrace and appreciate the love their husbands show. Do I agree with them? Absolutely- not! I want to marry someone who loves me just as much as I love him.

This is the revelation I think all women need to understand. When you love someone just as much as they love you, your love has room to grow and flourish. Due to the potential in flourishing, you can truly appreciate and love a man in any state he will be in.

Let's look at this spiritually first. Earlier in chapter two we discussed having a personal encounter with our king. It was brought to our attention that even in our worse states, Christ died for us, because of the love that He has for us.

When Jesus had a justifiable reason to reject us, He accepted every single one of our faults and remained on the course to Calvary. On that cross between two thieves, our Savior kept in mind every mistake we would ever make, and yet He never complained. In all the pain His physical body endured, His heart was hurting because He understood that He was also suffering and dying for those who would reject Him. Yet, our God, our

Lord and our Savior never complained. Why? His love for us is far greater than our faults, and He died for us, and later, He rose for us!

While you struggled with prostitution, drug addictions, alcoholism, stealing, lying, murder, hatred, insecurities and all that, God never stopped loving you. While you were in those states or states of mind, He never loved you any less. He has always looked at you with the purpose for which He created you. He may not have agreed with what you were doing, how you were doing it, and with the mindset you were doing it in, but God has always loved you.

Now naturally 'Ride or Die Chicks,' were not originally the women we associate them with now. Our men, no matter the ethnicity, are turning to women who can hold them down and love them in any state that they're in. The fathers and grandfathers of these men, use to find their 'ride or die chicks,' in the church! Think about it!

While your grandfathers may have been struggling with alcoholism, gambling, infidelity, your grandmother was holding down home. She never ceased in praying for her family. Most of the time your parents never knew that the mortgage payment was late, that daddy didn't come home, that mama was actually working two jobs, and she remained faithful in ministry.

I'm not stereotyping our men. The fact of the matter though, is when a mother tells her son he should go to the church to find him a wife, she knows that if the woman has a relationship with God, she is a true 'ride or die chick.' She will always be praying for her husband. She will be taking care of home. She has the capacity and desire to love him in any state. She will love him in the good times and the bad times.

Doesn't this sound like marriage vows? We are to love for better or for worse, for richer and for poorer, in sickness and in health, until death creates the separation. This goes back to the question, do you have love to offer?

What about joy, is that something you can offer? Having great pleasure or happiness constitutes having Joy. As a part of the fruit of the spirit, we have joy. How do we offer joy to others? We offer joy to other people by not bringing them misery.

I think we all can attest that there is at least one person in this world we have attempted to avoid because of the misery that they bring. The misery that accompanies their presence could be classified as anxiety, sorrow, discomfort, heartaches, headaches, tension, and other unpleasant feelings.

No matter how much God loves us, sometimes we too bring Him misery. A life filled with sin and disobedience will bring God misery. Although God's anger will last but a moment, the unintended consequences and associated feelings that sin and disobedience creates can last longer. We put ourselves in miserable situations and eventually attempt to find ways to cope with the guilt and shame.

Forgetting that our God is a healer and a deliverer we never seek Him to heal and deliver us. We attempt to apply the saying, 'time heals all wounds,' to our lives. Instead of being whole, we remain broken. We unfortunately attempt to carry this brokenness into relationships. As a woman, know that a man does not want to be miserable. When Mr. Right-for-you goes to God looking for you, he'll be looking for an escape. He will look to your comfort as a place free from stress, responsibility, judgment, and rejection. If you ever have known real joy, it's an escape from the concerns of life! It doesn't matter what is going on around you, the happiness you feel will be unexplainable. As a wife, you will sometimes have to be your husband's escape by exemplifying joy.

While having joy, can you provide joy in others people life? Can you bring about great feelings of pleasure and happiness? In order to do this, you have to be content with yourself. You have to know what it feels like to have joy in order to share that with someone else. If you don't, you'll go through life expecting people to make you happy. This leaves you open for great disappointment. Again being married then becomes an instrument to receive what you lack, instead of enhancing in someone else's life what is already there. A man cannot make you happy, especially if you don't know what makes you happy.

I love being pampered, but I've learned that if I don't pamper myself I can't expect my husband to do it for me. There are different levels of pampering. It was only in 2013 that I had my first massage. I was apprehensive about a complete stranger being in my personal space on that level, but that was the best eighty plus minutes of April 2013. I go and get pedicures, manicures, and occasionally I allow a professional to do my hair, that's different levels of pampering. I know what it feels like to cook breakfast for myself, and have breakfast in bed while I'm wrapped up in my fuzzy robe. That's naturally speaking. Spiritually, I know what it feels like to have God hear my prayers and answer them. Having a relationship with God brings me joy. It is a joy knowing that my faith in Him is not in vain.

I know what makes me happy or gives me joy. Do you? If you do, are you bringing yourself joy on a consistent basis? When is the last time you took yourself out for a steak dinner? When is the last time you didn't have to spend money to make yourself feel happy? When is the last time in your relationship with God that He made you smile, laugh, giggle, blush, and wish the moment would never end? Oh my! I can hear the Spirit saying, that we have work to do.

I had a conversation with my best friend, and I was telling her how in writing this book, I've enjoyed the journey and that dating really isn't on my agenda, despite the advances by some men. You know what she said to me? She said she was proud of me for dating myself.

In dating myself, which leads us into the next aspect of the fruit of the spirit, have I not only experienced real joy, but also peace. Oh yes! There is peace of mind, peace in my heart, and in the surrounding atmosphere.

When thinking of peace, we think tranquility or freedom from irritations, distractions, and nuisances. We are to not only possess peace, but also be peaceable.

Being open, because we are overcomers by the words of our testimony, this is one of the hardest things for me, being peaceable. I have a tendency to want to speak my mind, especially when someone attempts to speak over me, ignore me, undermine me, or belittle me. I will hold my peace, but only until I begin to burst at the seams with aggravation. The outcome is usually catastrophic, not only for myself, but for the other party involved.

I am a constant work in progress because God desires great from my life. He understands that no matter how much I desire peace, that sometimes I'm not the most peaceable. Sometimes I need to shut my mouth and allow Him to fight my battles.

What I truly admire about God is that He makes the process worth going through. He didn't bribe me, but He let me in on a secret. He enlightened me if you will, about my husband. He let me know that my yelling as I'm busting at the seams with aggravation isn't going sit well with my husband.

Some men will go into yelling wars with their wives because of ego. My husband on the other hand, will not be one of those men. My husband will probably shut me down before I get to that point, and guess what? I respect that. So I find it interesting how often God is refining me when it comes to being peaceable. There have been times when I have passed the test and times when I have failed. Until I consistently pass, God has to continue to break me down and rebuild me.

Being peaceable is not just avoiding yelling wars; it is using the finesse you were created with to keep harmony within any relationship including your future marriage. Sometimes it will require you to not say a word when you feel the need say what is on your mind. Being peaceable is swallowing your pride, and truly allowing God to fight your battless. Do you have to be a pushover? No. Being peaceable is executing wisdom.

Executing wisdom will allow you to be assertive. This means you don't need aggression in order to make a point.

It is hard to bring peace to someone else's life when you are battling spiritual unrest within yourself. Peace comes from being connected to the source of peace. When you've experienced real peace of mind, you fight to keep peace of mind.

That seems counterintuitive. Why would someone have to fight to keep peace of mind? We are living in a time when the enemy of our souls is playing for keeps. He understands that to have the mind of a person, inevitably is to have the person himself or herself. The bible tells us that we shouldn't conform to the thinking of this world, but we have to be transformed by the renewing of our mind. We are to take on the mind of Christ.

When we take on the mind of Christ we are kingdom minded. In being kingdom minded God will keep us in perfect peace. Being kingdom minded is to ultimately have our mind consistently on God! If our adversary, the devil is trying to take over our mind, it will be a battle worth fighting to keep our peace of mind.

Have you ever noticed someone who doesn't have peace in his or her life? You can feel the uneasiness, and it makes you uncomfortable. If you don't have peace within yourself, why take your uneasiness into a marriage and make your husband feel uncomfortable? Allow God to bring you to a place of peace. Isaiah 26:3-4 (KJV) verse 3 "Thou wilt keep him in perfect peace, whose mind is stayed on thee: because he trusteth in thee." Verse 4 "Trust ye in the Lord for ever: for in the Lord JEHOVAH is everlasting strength." God will bring you to a place of peace and keep you there if you keep your mind on Him. He truly has everything we need.

What do you have to offer? Is longsuffering on that list? Are you able to exhibit patience in the midst of adversity? Can you go through trials and tribulations without complaining?

I think this is hard for most Christians, especially those in my generation because we have a tendency to think that we are owed something. It doesn't stop with God. We think God owes us for being saved. We have a mindset that once we accept Him as our Lord and Savior our problems should stop.

This won't be the last time you hear it, but if Christ suffered why shouldn't we? 2 Timothy 3:12, (KJV) "Yea, and all that will live godly in Christ Jesus, shall suffer persecution." We are going to go through some things.

How we go through is becoming an issue. We are living in a time when it seems commonplace to complain about everything. Instead of being doers, we have become complainers. This is one of the reasons the salt is losing its savor!

God is tired of us complaining. The reason we aren't passing the taste test and God keeps sending us back to the kitchen for refining is because we haven't developed the right characteristics that are evidence of the fruit of the spirit. With each consecutive taste test, we are supposed to be getting better, not worse. Where are those who are longsuffering? This doesn't mean we cannot go to God with our problems. We're supposed to. He is a counselor. It is the whining in the midst of us forgetting whom God is, that causes us to fail the test.

The marked difference in longsuffering is patience during adversity. Are you able to endure afflictions, knowing that it is working out for your good? I think what is happening when we complain about trials and difficulties, is our failure to apply the word to our lives. I've heard a handful of ministers including my own pastor say "work the word." It is easier to go through hard times when you work the word!

If the only thing you can tell yourself is, 'it's working for my good,' hold on to that word until you see the fruit of your faith! The essence of faith is to see it before you see it.

You are somebodies wife! Therefore, it is required of you that you be longsuffering. Being married will require you to be patient with your husband. We will have to tolerate certain discomforts for a season within our marriages. You may marry someone who travels for work eighty percent of the workweek, and therefore, he doesn't have as much time to spend at home the first two or three years of your marriage. God desires for us to remain prayerful in that season, and give Him the opportunity to work it out in His timing; hence our need for patience. Remember no man is going to be perfect, just as you as a woman are not. We will have to be disciplined in executing patience in this midst of discomforts, especially if our husband is working our last nerve.

Earlier in this chapter I mentioned how we should use our finesse to avoid yelling wars. Operating in finesse goes beyond being peaceable, but also gentle. This is the next facet of the fruit of the spirit we will consider, gentleness.

To display gentleness simply means you are one that is less extreme or intense in your actions, reactions, and responses. As Christians, we shouldn't be flying off the hinges and becoming belligerent. Our mannerisms are supposed to be identifiably different. We are supposed to sanctify God in the eyes of the people.

We feel as though being gentle produces weakness. Factually speaking, it is this very mindset that produces weakness. To achieve discipline in one's mannerisms requires great strength. Being gentle, when your desire is to introduce your right palm to the left side of someone's face, requires great strength. You lovely ladies can pretend you have been saved all your life, but some of us have always had a little fight within us. Gentleness only comes, however, if you allow God to work in your life. Working the word is only going to do so much if you don't allow the word to work in you!

As a future wife, I realize and I hope you realize that your actions, reactions, and responses will require the working of your finesse. We are naturally gentler than men. We are viewed as the delicate counterpart. It is in our best interest to act accordingly.

One day, your husband may be angry and not because of you. More than likely, he isn't going to talk about it, because he doesn't have a desire to. Often times as women we attempt to push the issue immediately, and eventually beg them to open up to us. What then happens is his anger becomes slightly directed toward you. Proverbs 15:1 tells us that a "soft," or gentle answer turns away wrath. Gentleness goes a long way. Instead of prying, acknowledge his state and pray. Have regard for him, not his condition.

Give your husband time to calm down first, then sashay your cute self toward him and work the finesse God instilled within you! Sometimes you won't be able to do that, but as I stated earlier it takes wisdom. Sometimes he'll just want to be left alone for a moment. A gentle woman won't lose control over her mouth and attack him for such a simple request. She will however, intercede on her husband's behalf. She may also rub his back and massage his feet. Oh my! There are different ways to minister to your husband.

Goodness, well that goes without saying. How hard is it to be good if "the old man" is passed away? The old you will not pass away until you deny yourself, pick up your cross and follow Christ. Denying yourself comes with a disciplined life; a life filled with prayer, fasting and the studying of God's word. There is nothing wrong with possessing and displaying high moral standards.

As a matter of fact, the word of God tells us to keep His commandments. We aren't to turn to the left or to the right. When you develop a relationship with God, you'll know what is morally correct and incorrect. Being good goes beyond relationships; God desires for us to be honest and have integrity. We shouldn't, as Christians be the ones demonstrating dishonesty by stealing, taking bribes, and being corrupt. We serve an incorruptible God; we either love God or shun sin, or we love sin and shun God. Matthew 6:24 (KJV) "No man can serve two masters; for either you will hate the one, and love the other; or else he will hold to the one and despise the other. Ye cannot serve God and mammon." Are you morally sound?

Sometimes we have good intentions, but we end up doing badly no matter how good our intentions were. For example, your friend Malik doesn't have a place to stay because his house flooded due to the weather. Instead of using the discount code provided by your job, which is available to friends and family for a hotel, you offer him to stay at your house. Malik isn't saved, but he says he's a believer. He brings alcohol into your home, and you've been sober for however long you've been delivered. He coaxes you into having one glass. One glass turns into four and now you're wondering why a good friend is starting to look like a last supper.

Will you be able to bring goodness or excellence to your marriage?

Oh ye of little faith! Do you have faith to offer to God? Whether you decide to marry or not, all your faith should be in God. This means all your confidence and trust should be in God. Proverbs 3:5 (KJV) "Trust in the

Lord with all thine heart; and lean not unto thine own understanding." To not lean on your own intellect requires that all your trust be in God.

We have faulty thinking! As women, sometimes our thinking and judgment are clouded by our sentiments or our moods. We as women, we don't have to be drunk to say things we don't mean; we can simply be emotionally unbalanced to say some off the wall stuff. I'm not saying we're crazy, I'm merely saying we often speak our mind without a clear frame of mind. WE have faulty thinking.

This is why we are to trust God with all our heart. We have to have total faith in Him, God, who is far from faulty in His thinking.

When God does allow you to one day marry, realize that we are never to take our faith in God and put it in our husbands. Faith in your husband is not the same thing as having faith in God.

To have faith in your husband means that you acknowledge the gift(s) and vision(s) that God has placed inside of him; and you realize the height he can soar in God. That same faith will help you realize that if God allowed him to, your husband would be able to conquer the world. Faith in your husband is identifying his effectiveness within the body of Christ, within your community and family and providing support and the stability he needs to maintain his effectiveness. Having faith in your husband is not the same as having faith in your God.

Faith in God allows us to look at an empty refrigerator and say, "thank you God for being Jehovah Jireh, my God who provides." Faith in God allows us to say, "I am healed," when you've been diagnosed with a terminal illness. When the enemy comes in like a flood, faith allows us to say, "God didn't bring me this far just to leave me."

As Christian women, our faith requires us to be constantly dependent upon God. There is no way you can translate your faith in God to faith in your husband. That is setting yourself up for a total disaster. Say goodbye to all the love, joy, peace, longsuffering, gentleness, and goodness you'd have already invested into the relationship. By attempting to even have such a great faith in man makes him an idol. God is not going to compete for your attention. He will not have any other gods beside Him!

If you are truly dependent upon God, please know that when the time is right, God will open that door for you to meet the man He has for you; that's if you haven't already.

Let's explore meekness as we further journey through the fruit of the spirit. Meekness can be equated with submissiveness. Have you yielded yourself over to God? To be kingdom minded is to ask God what does He desire for you to do. When He tells you, you are to execute, and if you are not sure how, you ask. This is a sore spot because we have our own agendas. We are expecting God to get in tuned with our scheduled programming

I'm guilty. My plan was to be married by twenty-five, first child by twenty-seven and another every two years until I reached eight children. Mind you, one of those pregnancies had to result in twins. I planned to be out of med school with my M.D./ Ph.D. by thirty, and own my own world-renowned OBGYN practice by thirty-six. This was my scheduled programming.

I've heard it phrased so many different ways, but there's a phrase that says, ' if you want to make God laugh, tell Him your plans.' God has gotten a great deal of laughter out of me. God has torn my agenda into pieces.

 However, setting aside my stubbornness and my pride, all I've ever had to do is seek God about the agenda He's created for my life. He's brought it to my attention that I could have been married to my Mr. Right-for-me a while ago, but I've been too persistent in attempting in telling Him how things ought to be. Therefore, He's allowed me to dabble in His permissive will, but enough is enough.

I'm done with God's permissive will. I want what He desires for my life, His divine will. I'm twenty-seven at the moment, but I'm knocking on twenty-eight's door. I don't have the time anymore to be frolicking as though I'm eighteen. I had a plan, but God has a plan.

He allowed me to graduate Magna Cum Laude from a prestigious HBCU. I only took part of my own agenda seriously and none of God's, therefore I also graduated less than a month away from my due date. The time I could have been spending working on my dual degree, I've been spending raising my beautiful daughter as a single mother.

The joys I desired to have with a husband as we raised our children together are non-existent. Instead, many nights I have watered my pillows with tears. Why? I attempted to get God to be in tuned with my agenda. That is not how it works. I am a creation who was supposed to submit herself to the creator.

Likewise with you, God is looking for meekness. Submit yourself completely over to God. Every desire, ambition, goal, and dream we need to yield over to God. Once we have done that, we need to ask, "God, now what would you have me to do?" It seems simple enough, but we struggle being dependent upon and submissive to God when we are used to being in control, and dependent upon ourselves.

Once I began to be open with God in how I loved being independent, and how being dependent on Him was difficult, God allowed situations in my life that required me to be dependent upon Him. Inevitably it made me meeker.

In relation to God, I realized my own inadequacies and His sovereignty. It all has been a humbling experience. You have to allow God to do the transformation in your life.

One day, when you're married, you will realize the importance in having learned to submit to God first. It will make submission to your husband easier.

I hear a lot of women talking about how they 'ain't' submitting to 'no' man. The conversation usually continues along this path; ' we are no longer living in the 1950's. I work and bring home just as much money. He needs to be cooking me dinner, and ironing my clothes.' Some husbands are fine with domestic work. That's not the point that is being made.

We in today's society have gravitated away from the natural order of things. God is the head. The husband is the head of the house. We are supposed to submit ourselves unto our husbands as unto to the Lord. Does this mean we have no voice? No it doesn't, but be respectful when you speak to him. Does it mean we can't contribute to our home? That is far from what it means to be submissive to your husband. To be submissive means your husband governs you. He provides the structure, the stability, and the checks and balances if you will that maintain your home.

Finally, this leads us into temperance. Temperance is the execution of self-restraint. If you've ever struggled with a temptation or an addiction you can appreciate God allowing the development of self-control or restraint.

To demonstrate self-control or restraint marks growth and maturity. In order to grow and mature requires that we crucify this flesh daily. Sometimes you will have to tell yourself, no!

We should be able to minister to those in the world without finding ourselves drawn to go back into the same sins we were delivered from. We are the light; we draw and are not drawn of this world.

There are many ways to exercise self-restraint. Not spending erratically, especially when one day you're expecting a fairytale wedding. Who's going to pay for it? You want to buy a house, but you've failed to save $500/month on your six-year plan to cover a portion of your down payment. You desire to go back to school, but you watch reality television when you should be studying.

You want to be married to a real good man, but you can't seem to say no to the type you've dated all your life. You feel that you've fasted and prayed long enough not to get tempted to sleep with him, and instead of telling him your body belongs to God until you're married, you hope his layaway plan will eventually result in marriage, along with his salvation.

Oh yes, it's real. My type is not tall, dark, and handsome, but for some women whose type is, self-restraint, if you play on the enemies' territory, will eventually become non-existent, if you are constantly flirting with Mr. Tall-dark-and-handsome.

I don't want a man on layaway. What does that mean? I don't want to have to give installments of my body, my time, my money, and my energy in order to wait months, and years to have some man who isn't even moving in the same direction that I am. Self-restraint goes a long way!

When Mr. Right-for-me comes looking for me, I will not have to give installments of myself and hope he accepts me for who I am. I am determined to wait on God. I realize that no matter how fine, sexy, smart, intelligent and flirtatious some men may be, none of them compare to the man that God has for me! So daily, I ask God to help me and to keep me, because not only do I want all of the God I can get, I want to be ready and available for my husband! So I exercise self-control daily!

Is it hard? Sometimes. I'm being completely honest. I don't have everything all figured out, because I'm not God. However, I do live in this fleshly body, and it has a mind of its own. It will get you caught up if you allow yourself to be drawn away by lust. In my own life, I've compromised way too much in the past to ever want to take another risk and miss out on what God has for me. If I forget this fact, yes, it gets hard. But when I realize that nothing profitable can ever come from compromising instead of waiting for God's best, it's a piece of cake.

When you have self-control and God blesses you with a husband it is easier to embody other characteristics such as faithfulness! Since we're already talking about faithfulness within a marriage, let's labor here for a moment.

The last thing I'd ever want to do is marry the man beyond my dreams and be unfaithful to him. Faithfulness goes beyond being committed, dedicated and devoted to one man sexually. We are emotional beings. To invest our emotions into a man other than our husbands can be just as detrimental as sleeping with another man.

You know there are some things you would be uncomfortable with your husband doing. One of those things would be confiding in another woman. The cold part about that, however, is men do not get as easily and emotionally attached to women as women do men. We chastise men because of an emotional attachment a woman will have on them. Therefore, we simply ask them not to talk to women. What makes you think your husband would appreciate you confiding in another man when you make emotional attachments?

Let's explore this spiritually. God wants all of you. He says to love Him first with every fiber of your being. We are to acknowledge God in all things. We are to draw close to Him, so that God can draw closer to us. What do we do?

If we have problems it seems as though God is our last resort. After attempting to figure it out on our own, we ask mama, daddy, granny, our best friends, co-workers, pastors, and everybody else what we should do about our problems. If we had acknowledged God first, He would have directed our path. We prolong our problems by putting our trust in other people. That's not being faithful to God.

Commitment requires constant consideration. When we consider God, we think of how He might feel toward our actions or inactions. In making decisions we desire for God to be pleased with us, therefore, we recognize His omniscience and realize He has the answers we seek. Being mindful of the God we serve, we don't want to disappoint Him; as a matter of fact, when we are committed to God, we seek to make Him happy.

We cannot be considerate of God when we are attempting to get something out of Him. Our goal should never be to use God instead of love Him. That will always be a losing battle. Understand that when you sincerely love God and are committed to Him, God will sustain you. All your needs will be met! And because of your dedication to Him, God will throw in your wants as well.

Faithfulness is a true expression of love. Even when an opportunity to turn away from God presents itself, because of your love toward Him, because of how much He loves you, because of what God has delivered you from, nothing would ever be worth compromising that. Nothing! This is the level of relationship God desires for us to reach with Him; real love, a.k.a. faithfulness!

At this depth in God, we can show mercy. Being recipients of God's mercy, we understand that we weren't deserving of the leniency that was given to us. The love God has toward us softened the punishment we were destined to receive for our sins and disobedience. As Christians, we are to extend that mercy to those who offend us.

Sometimes those offenses will come in our marriages. We never expect to feel neglected, lonely, misunderstood, or grievously disappointed in a marriage that God has preordained; but it happens.

We as women assume that because we've dated a man longer than three months that he should remember everything there is to know about us. It'll get worse once you get married, consequently. Your husband will be bound to forget something important that you feel he shouldn't. It's never because he wanted to forget; most men do not have the capacity for technicalities and particulars. What eventually happens is we leave room for the enemy to rear his head in our marriages by assuming we married mind readers.

Your husband will be observant enough to recognize when you're upset, but you're expecting him to know why without verbally communicating to him. Offenses will come. Not all will be intentional. Whether some are, it's up to us to operate with mercy. This goes back when we debunked the title Mr. Right; when you expect your husband to be perfect, you marry presuming he will never offend you. What happens when he does? Marriage is not something you should take lightly, and decide to run from when it doesn't look like how you imagined.

Be compassionate and understanding. When you begin to look at others judgmentally, you forget that could easily be you. This is where humility should be prevalent, and yet it's lacking in marriages.

After a business you invested a great portion of your savings in, goes bankrupt after ten years, you'd want your significant other to be compassionate, and understand why you are slightly discouraged. If you were to become sick, and not a seasonal cold sick, but knocking at deaths door sick, you'd want your spouse to be understanding why you don't feel well enough to walk through the park to spend some quality time.

We should be supportive. As a helpmeet, we are helpful. We induce confidence, reveal hope, stimulate productivity, assist, and help strengthen preexisting goals, dreams, aspirations, and aid in the development of new ones.

So I ask this question, are you a liability or an asset? If you were to meet Mr. Right-for-you tomorrow, will he be able to see the blessing you will be in his life? Will you bring strength and virtue to his life? Are you an asset?

Maybe you are an asset in development. This means that God is reconstructing your life to make you a suitable asset.

This leads us into our next discussion on where God has you housed.

Be Held

Considering our analogy of a restaurant and a menu, where does God have you housed? Are you available to "be held" for viewing when Mr. Right-for-you walks in? Is God still perfecting what you have to offer? Is God on His final draft, therefore you're ready for the printer, or to be sealed?

If God is yet taste testing, and you haven't allowed God to perfect certain characteristic within you that He desires to put on the menu for His and Mr. Right-for-you enjoyment, you haven't been to the printer yet.

God will not put anything into ink until He knows you are ready. There is a quote by Benjamin Franklin that states, "If you fail to plan, you are planning to fail." Marriage is no different. You have to plan for marriage before you meet the groom. Without planning for marriage in advance, you are setting yourself up for failure.

As the menu, you are the center stage. Mr. Right-for-you is coming to look for you because you have something to offer him. It cannot be reiterated enough, you have something within you that was created specifically for him, and vice versa. However, if you never allow God to perfect in you what Mr. Right-for-you needs, you both lose out.

We've discussed how the fruit of spirit amongst other characteristics aid us in our future marriages. This however, is only a portion of the preparation.

Who are you? Do you know? Some men are attracted to insecure women because they are easy to take advantage of. Those same men aren't looking for permanence. We are Christian women, but we struggle with insecurities, and some of us have fallen victim to men who only wanted to take advantage of our insecurities.

It's easy to fall for a man who calls you beautiful every day when you don't realize that whether he says it or not, you are beautiful. It's easy to get attached to a man who prays for you, encourages you, and makes you smile and laugh. If you don't know what it feels like to have God answer your prayers, what it feels like to encourage yourself, to do things that make you smile and laugh; you'll fall for a man who is simply preying on your weaknesses. Some men operate under the auspices of the church to advance their hidden agendas, and some women fall prey because they weren't praying!

Know who you are in God, and if you are unsure, the answer is just a few prayers away. If you struggle with insecurities realize that this is not how God created you to be. He will strengthen and fortify you to be a woman of high esteem.

While some men are attracted to insecure women as a means to prey on them, some men are attracted to women who we label as insecure when they are simply humble. I love a song by John Legend titled, "You & I (Nobody In the World)." In the song he starts off singing how the woman he loves spends time to intricately fix her makeup, he sings "guess you don't know that you're beautiful." Just a couple of seconds later he sings, "and if your mirror won't make it any clearer, I'll be the one to let you know…" she's the only woman for him. Towards the end of the song he even tells her that she doesn't even have to try, "you don't have to try. Don't try, don't try…"

A woman who recognizes she is beautiful, but still humbly down plays just how beautiful she is, is not insecure at all. She knows who she is, but she also recognizes whose she is. Beautiful women reading this book, find your place in God. When you've found it, be confident in who God has created you to be. Once you've embraced it, you won't have to announce it! Confidence speaks for itself, just like success.

What other preparation have you made? As a vessel of God, preparation includes consecration. Since we are to appeal to God first, what are you doing to set yourself apart to be a vessel meet for the masters' use?

In my personal life, I've noticed that when I watch a lot of drama on television I get quite dramatic. What makes that so bad is I'm dramatic without reality television. However, when I've had a television marathon, I am far less peaceable. I remember going on a TV fast once. There was a considerable difference within the first week. Not just in my attitude but in my productivity as well. If you are full of something other than the spirit of God, you don't have room for Him. You can pray all you want for a move of God in your life, but He will not move until you make room for Him to move!

Not only does God need room to move, you also have to be in position to receive what God has. Giving God room to move is not the same as being in position for the move of God.

When God is ready to move in your life, giving Him room to move means that there is nothing in your life that is competing with Him. Nothing should be competing with God for your attention, your time, your money, your heart, or your body. That list could be longer, but you understand.

Being in position means you've already removed all obstacles, and now you are putting yourself in a strategic place spiritually, mentally, emotionally, and physically to be receptive of what God has for you.

This is usually when revisions take place, when you position yourself to receive them. James 1:2-4 (KJV) verse 2 "My brethren, count it all joy when ye fall into divers temptation;" Verse 3 "Knowing this, that the trying of your faith worketh patience." Verse 4 "But let patience have her perfect work, that ye may be perfect and entire, wanting nothing." We are to allow patience to have its perfect work in us. Why? Through patience we are perfected; we become whole and we'll lack nothing.

We'll never be without flaws. It's our goal, but we are to let God do the perfecting. When patience has worked in us through the trying of our faith, patience will work out what doesn't belong. Revisions. We are continually being transformed into the image of Christ.

As discussed earlier, some of us women have been through a lot in our lives. We've picked up some unwanted baggage along the way. Let's be honest, no one really wants to have anger, harbor hurt, un-forgiveness, doubt, bitterness, and negativity for years. Who wants to struggle with lust, promiscuity, lying, hatred and distrust?

This will weigh you down, shackle your faith and hinder you from embracing a real relationship with God. Do you want to have a successful marriage with the man God created for you? If you don't get rid of bondage, you risk destroying the relationship in its infancy.

When patience has had its perfect work in us, we can be entire. Entire means whole; or with no part left out. Being further simplified we'll be free from voids. When we allow the trials of life to try our faith and allow patience to work in us, fundamentally we are permitting God to fill the voids. Voids are created when the baggage is worked out of our lives.

If baggage has been worked out, something needs to be worked in. Isaiah 61:3 (KJV) "To appoint unto them that mourn in Zion, to give unto them beauty for ashes, the oil of joy for mourning, the garment of praise for the spirit of heaviness; that they might be called trees of righteousness, the planting of the Lord, that he might be glorified." Verse 4 "And they shall build the old waste, they shall raise up the former desolations, and they shall repair the waste cities, the desolations of many generations."

For all that you have endured, the temptations, the trying of your faith, of your patience, for the hurt, scorn, abuse, amongst whatever else that has caused you to be despondent, God shall restore you and make you better. Certainly "the glory of this latter house shall be greater than the former."

Be assured that you will be entire with God's love, His joy, peace, hope, faith, zeal, passion, positivity and so much more. This reminds me of that fruit to be desired, the fruit of the spirit.

When God has filled all empty slots in your life, you will want for nothing! This is powerful, because God will always be enough. This is why it is so important we seek the kingdom of God first! With any relationship, it is a process and it takes quality time with our King.

When God is enough, anything He blesses you with will be enough. What is my advice? Trust the process. There is no failure in God. He will not fail you, and if you yield to Him, you will not fail God. When you get to a place in God when He knows you are ready for that next step, you truly will be something to behold!

I don't know about you, but I want God to perfect me to where He is pleased with me. I want God to look at me and smile. I want God to wait in anticipation for me to wake up in the morning because He loves hearing from me. We don't think that our God operates in this manner, but believe you me, He does. Have you ever woken up in the middle of the night and couldn't go back to sleep and you began to pray? Hours go by before you realize how much time has passed. God loves that quality time.

It's been said many times and in many ways, God desires your heart first. Once He can entrust you with loving someone else, He'll put you into ink. Where are you housed?

What About You

There hasn't really been a dedicated section of this book where we've discussed what you stand to gain from a marriage. This should be self-explanatory. We've explored little by little thus far how you have to have something to offer.

Often times we wonder, well what about Mr. Right-for-me; does he have to go through the process that I must go through? Of course he does. Why would God require you to prepare to be receptive of a blessing that carries himself more like a curse? How your husband needs to prepare himself for marriage depends on who he is. He may have gone through a lot more than you would have ever imagined. All you'll see is the final product.

However, before we jump ahead of ourselves, let's consider the establishment of the relationship with God. What about us? We appeal to God first, but -what about us?

I think this is my favorite part of the book. Are you ready? Drum roll please… establishing a relationship with God means you have the heart of God! Not that you transform to have the heart of God, although, this too is true, but God's heart is yours. You will have His undivided attention. This is our payoff for becoming all that God desires of us.

If you aren't connected to God in the first place this doesn't seem like much. If you are connected you realize that this is worth more than the world itself. In actuality, it's priceless. This is where the children of Israel missed out time and time again.

God loved their forefathers so much that He promised that their children's children would be blessed. He promised Abraham that his decedents would be like the sand on the seashore, innumerable!

The children of Israel had the very God who created the heavens and the earth and all that's within it at their fingertips. He was talking to them out of burning bushes, raining manna from heaven and turning bitter water sweet. They were His people, and God wanted to show Himself to be their God who loved them.

When Christ came to redeem, He didn't count us out. Therefore, what He offered the Jews, He has offered us. We have an all access pass through Christ Jesus! I have an equal opportunity to have the heart of God. When we love God first, God not only opens up His heart to us but His mind.

1 Corinthians 2:9 (KJV) "But as it is written, Eye hath not seen, nor ear heard, neither have entered into the heart of man, the things that God hath prepared for them that love him." What you think God will do is not even comparable to what He will do when you love Him like you've never loved anybody.

Have you ever seen a man so in love with a woman, that he'd do anything for her? She lives a pampered life, and she doesn't hesitate in pampering him with her love. Our relationship with God is the same. God is so in love with us that it is everlasting. He loves us so much that He'd do anything for us. He doesn't give this much love or favor to the angels.

Think about it this way; God is the creator of everything. God is the source of all life. When you enter into a cherished relationship with God, and you learn to love Him like there is no tomorrow, everything He has becomes yours without limit. There is nothing we need that God doesn't have. There is nothing you want that He is not able to provide. Everything you could think of is at your disposal. He's making provisions now that you don't even see. What I find to be crazy is that you really never seek to have stuff, when you have God. When God is your everything, material possessions, status, and titles become insignificant.

When we learn to love God for simply being God, He will literally give us the world. We mean more than this world does to Him. When we love Him with a genuine love, we give God our world. We put ourselves in a position to receive His best. How do I know it's His best? First off, God operates in excellence and splendor. Anything contradictory to this is contradictory to His character! He never changes, therefore, the same God who was elaborate in the creation of this universe, still is elaborate.

Secondly, if you truly love someone in the natural, you'll go through great lengths to show your love. If you could, and you knew they wouldn't take advantage of your love, you'd spoil them with anything they wanted. Likewise with God in the spiritual; when you genuinely love God, God knows you will not take advantage of Him. Without hesitation, He will give you His best both spiritually and naturally. Psalms 37:4 (KJV) "Delight thyself also in the LORD; and he shall give thee the desires of thine heart."

Well, what are God's best spiritual blessings? There are a host of blessings, but let's look at few. One of my favorites is answered prayer. The benefit of making God the first priority is answered prayers. For me, I feel humbled and glad that God both heard my prayer and answered my prayer. What I find even more amazing is when I've been praying for someone, and they begin talking about the very thing I've been praying about and it confirms that God is working.

To know that God hears me, oh my, I can't even articulate how that really makes me feel. The God who is in control of everything proves Himself to me every time I kneel down in prayer, by confirming He has heard me and that He is working because of my relationship. I want to encourage you amazing women reading this book that might be thinking, 'I don't really have that deep of a relationship.' Girl, it doesn't have to be deep, you just need a desire! If you take the initiative, God will prove Himself just to boost your faith. Eventually, initiative will flourish into communion with God!

For the longest time, I've been fearful about operating in the gifts that God has placed inside of me. It is not that I don't think I can do it; I just don't have all the formal training. So I've sat on my gifts waiting for the opportunity to receive the appropriate license for this, and the green light to do that. My current work schedule has never permitted me the opportunity to have formal training. The Holy Spirit helped me realize that this was a poor excuse to sit down on God's best gifts! Even if I never received the proper training, Jesus was not a licensed evangelist. He followed the leading of God and that's the best protocol to have. Some of you reading this book are sitting on some of God's best gifts and refuse to operate in them. But God obviously trusts you enough to invest them within you.

If you have to prophesy to yourself until you can exercise that gift at your home church, then girl, do what you got to do. If you have to lay hands on your mother to pray for healing, do you! He's given you the gift, now work the gift. Even if you aren't operating at the level you think you can operate, ask God to show you how to work the gift at the level where you are.

If He's given you a gift, He's definitely going to bless you with an anointing and some power. There is a level of power for everybody, but when God gifts or bestows supernatural power on you, that's giving you the best of Himself. God's power lies within His word, and if His word is in you, you have His power. The anointing is the outpouring that enables us to operate effectively, using the power to function at the capacity by which God has called us.

Not only will God grace you with the best of His gifts, power and anointing, but God will simply favor your life. According to Deuteronomy 28:2 "And all these blessings shall come on thee, and overtake thee, if thou shalt hearken unto the voice of the LORD thy God."

I remembered when I interviewed for Amtrak; I prayed that the favor of God would go before me. As a result, based on my interview alone, I was their first choice. I had recently been in a car accident and I was unable to accept the position right away. God had granted me so much favor that they held my position until I was able to work. That is nothing compared to the greater that God has in store for me.

Grace is a different form of favor. It's unmerited, which means it is a favor that you cannot earn. However, when you have a relationship with God and He approves of your lifestyle, He will be preferential towards you. When you hearken or listen to His leading, when you desire and seek after Him, what God has for you will overtake you! Have you considered what that means?

To overtake is to overrun. My favorite definitions that I found for overtake included coming suddenly and unexpectedly, or to affect suddenly and powerfully! God's best means that His blessings will come suddenly. He'll bless us with things we weren't looking for. There is nothing ordinary about the God we serve! Therefore, His blessings will have powerful or extravagant effects. When God's blessings overtake you, your response will not be subtle. When you truly love God you are not fearful to show your appreciation. Definitely be humble, but never feel ashamed to magnify your God.

I'm sure you can think of the best you desire spiritually within your life. What is amazing about God, is that it's not just His spiritual blessings that will overtake you; it's the natural blessings too!

Marriage serves a dual purpose. It has a spiritual element and a natural element. Looking from this perspective helps us to realize that marriage, although it serves a higher purpose, is truly a bonus! It is in fact the giving of God's best both naturally and spiritually.

I want to be prepared to receive God's best. What is meant for me, I want it! I'm not going to assume that because it hasn't happened yet, that it never will. I realize that until I started writing this book, I've never really prepared to be married. I've enjoyed the thought, and I've prayed about how I've wanted to be married, but I have never prepared to make room for another person in my life.

In my spiritual walk with God, when I put in the effort I see the transformation, the change, the maturity. When I love God, I prepare myself to love someone else. When I allow the love of God to take permanent residence within me, I prepare to receive the love of another.

I've prayed about God sending that great man my way, one who is perfect for me, but I have to allow the perfect God to prepare me for that man. While so much has been focused on what God is looking for and what Mr. Right-for-you is searching for, understand that you get all that you could ever want. For me, it's greater than simply waking up to a man every morning.

I find joys in simple things. So the fact that my husband will look at me like he loves me and adores me, that is what I want and look forward to. The fact that we could spend hours talking and laughing about God knows what, I want that, and I look forward to it. For my husband to recognize that I'm in a bad space or feeling sick and he comes and prays for me- oh I want that and I look forward to it.

You are an amazing woman, and God has a plan for your life. My end of the chapter prayer is that God begins to reveal to you the true asset that you are.

Dear heavenly father, there is truly no one like you. You are a great and mighty God. We understand that you desire the best out of us, and you desire the best for us. God, we thank you for the process because in the process, you make us complete. When we are complete in you, we'll have no lack! God complete us. Fill the voids with your comfort, your love, your peace, and your assurance. God perfect the work that you have begun in each and every one of us. God be all that we need. Quench the thirst and satiate the desires that we don't understand. We patiently wait on you, because you bless with the best gifts. We know that in your timing, you will bring us into a season of overflow. Your spiritual and natural blessings will overtake us. There will be no sorrow in what you bless us with. We thank you in advance for the man you will bring into our lives. We trust and believe that we will receive all that we need from you and will be blessed with all we could ever want from him. Thank you! In Jesus name we pray, Amen!

Chapter

7

The Owner

———————

*L*et's get it out the way now; how successful is our God? How often and how well does our God get the job done? How can you even ask that question? You should be ashamed of yourselves. Okay, maybe you weren't thinking this directly, however, this is the question we simultaneous ask with, "where is my husband?" We assume that God hasn't done this before. We'll look to online dating sites before we wait on our perfect God to do a perfect work in us. Say what?

If we compare man to God, we find that there is no comparison. Our God is great at what He does. However, when it comes to people, nothing is ever 100%. As stated previously, people are fickle and waver. A person's ambition will change over the course of their lifetime. People lie about whom they are. This is why blind dates sometimes end in disappointment. On-line dating sites will leave you hopeless. However, if you have true faith in God, you understand and realize that He is constant and consistent.

If you were wondering, our God has a 100% success rate. I know because God's word is solid. Let us look at two scriptures to support this. Numbers 23:19 (KJV) "God is not a man, that he should lie; neither the son of man, that he should repent: hath he said, and shall he not do it? or hath he spoken, and shall he not make it good?" Isaiah 55:10-11(KJV) vs. 10 "For as the rain cometh down, and the snow from heaven, and returneth not thither, but watereth the earth, and maketh it bring forth and bud, that it may give seed to the sower, and bread to the eater:" vs. 11 "So shall my word be that goeth forth out of my mouth: it shall not return unto me void, but it shall accomplish that which I please, and it shall prosper in the thing whereto I sent it."

How is this relevant? Well, when God has spoken something, because of who He is, it has to come to pass! If God has promised you something, believe that He's spoken it. A fulfilled promise is a checkpoint, which God gives us to let us know we've been operating within His will. God will always keep His end of the promise. Think about it. We only receive the promise when we uphold our end of the agreement. When you yield to the will of God and love Him, nothing can hinder the plan that God has for your life except a closed-mind. We'll talk about what a closed-mind is later.

If marriage is one of the promises God has made to you, rest assured that it has been spoken. Now you must wait for God's word to go forward and to accomplish that that pleases Him. Part of that word going forth is making sure that you are in a position to be receptive, a process, and that the man God has for you is also in position. Besides, God is the perfect matchmaker. He knows what kind of woman a man needs and vice versa.

God is omniscient! He knows the perfect combination of one man and one woman that will join together to create on flesh. Mark 10:6-9(KJV) Verse 6 "But from the beginning of the creation God made them male and female." vs. 7 "For this cause shall a man leave his father and mother, and cleave to his wife;" vs. 8 "And they twain shall be one flesh; so then they are no more twain but one flesh." vs. 9 "What therefore God hath joined together, let no man put asunder." This is imperfect math to us, but God is almighty! He knows what He is doing. God created all of us from the precision of His thoughts. His thoughts about marriage have just as much detail.

How then could you account for two people joining together to become one? It's hard not to address this at this juncture, but vaguely; if you don't recognize the importance of you one day operating as one in a marriage now, you'll marry selfishly. That is a recipe for a fiasco. Everything is not always going to be about you! Realize now, that you and your husband may come from completely different backgrounds. You two were raised differently and understand the world differently. Marriage is about forging a relationship where you not only begin to think but also operate cohesively with one another.

Since God, not man, has a 100% success rate, it brings us to this next point; every married couple, whether Christian or not is not in a God ordained marriage. I've noticed that, those who are, keep people in awe because we serve an awesome God! Have you ever noticed the chemistry between a husband and wife in a marriage that you know without a doubt is God ordained? It is cataclysmic! They flow well with each other. There are examples everywhere!

These marriages, despite rough patches still resemble fairytales. In these marriages, a husband could have a disagreement with his wife, and yet illuminate with joy and love moments later when she walks in the room. Believe it! In God ordained marriages, a wife can be disappointed with her husband, but never fails to remain passionate and appreciative of him. So you answer the question, has God done this before? I'll answer for you; yes God has. As a matter of fact, God is an expert!

There are couples that have been married for years. Not simply ten years, but thirty and forty plus years. Most of them are full of wisdom. How often do we go and seek it out? To say you want a good man is one thing, but are you ready and have you prepared to spend the rest of your life with that good man? That is how successful and efficient our God is.

As a sidebar, often times we don't prepare for long-term success because we can't think beyond our current state. In your spiritual walk, how often are you keeping in mind that you are working towards eternal life? As single women, we often complain about being single and we say we want a man, but how many of us are truly ready to spend the rest of our lives with one man? We speak from the present, but God works from the future. While we are praying for a husband, pray and ask God to give you the mindset for a long-term and permanent marriage.

God is the owner of this fine establishment, and He's omniscient. He knows what you and the consumer want. God has been in tuned with our desires well before we were conceived. God knew what He wanted us to be, and He derived a divine algorithm based on His thoughts of us while your mother was becoming the apple of your fathers' eye. We were once just a thought in the mind of God, but He knew that the right combination of your mother and father with certain allelic recombination's, you would exist.

Jeremiah 1: 4-5 Verse 4 "Then the word of the Lord came unto me, saying," Verse 5 "Before I formed thee in the belly I knew thee; and before thou camest forth out of the womb I sanctified thee, and I ordained thee a prophet unto the nations." WE are no different. You were created specifically for this time, with a purpose.

If God knew us before our parents knew we were coming, why wouldn't our amazing God know what the consumer wants? We forget that God is aware of every ordeal in our lives we attempt to hide or flaunt. One strand of our hair does not fall without Him knowing.

Mr. Right-for-you just as you, does not know what he wants half the time, but God is aware of our un-uttered desires.

Understand that the owner in His magnificence is not superficial. He didn't create one man for one woman simply because you two would look cute together. Marriage serves a higher purpose. Sure, at first glimpse, we see two people each unique, which are madly in love with each other. We admire their friendship and flirtatious attitude toward one another. I'm speaking of real God centered marriages, not drive through ones. We often see their union, without seeing their purpose.

It has already been established that marriage unites two dedicated Christians together as one. There are exceptions, but God emphasis are for Christian women waiting for Christian men. Moving along. What were these two dedicated people doing before they got married? Working for God! What did they become after they got married? A power couple!

Every Christian working in their gifts, which marries another Christian operating in their gifts, fortifies the other. Their gifts complement the others. Together, God will give them a vision to work towards. Marriage is about kingdom building. Again, we can't see that because the only thing we are looking for is a need to be met, your desire to be the receiver. You were created to meet a need, and that will not change once you are married. It will be heightened!

Marriage at this point shouldn't seem unimportant or undesirable. Adding this aspect of marriage should make it more attractive. Since my gifts will complement my husbands, he won't have a hard time understanding my need to consecrate. He will not have a problem with me attending 6 a.m. prayer at the church. Likewise, because his gifts will complement mine, I won't get upset when he tells me he has been asked to preach a revival in

Washington, D.C.. Our gifts will complement each other, and therefore, will we not only share a love for each other, but for God and for ministry.

Can you imagine late night pillow talk? It won't simply be about the foolishness going on in the world. It will go beyond talking about how your day was at work. You both can pick each other's brains about scripture. Now I may be the only woman right now excited about this, but when you love God and you study His word, to be able to share with your spouse the excitement from the revelation that God has given you, that's toe curling. To be able to pray with my husband one day, OMG! I love praying, but to be honest, when I started thinking of a husband and wife praying together I thought that would be awkward. That's not something you hear a lot of married couples say that they do together. But! When I realized the power and the covering that comes with a husband and wife praying together, oh I get excited now!

As Christian women reading this book, this is why it is so important that we realize that marriage is more than being justified to have sex. Marriage has a purpose seated in the heart of God that goes far beyond copulation. It is easy to talk about marriage from a carnal perspective, which would explain why divorce rates are skyrocketing.

Marriage is a part of a greater plan. Part of this same plan was simply for God to show His love toward us. This was always on God's itinerary. If you look at the Bible as a whole, it is a love story. By doing a work for God in ministering to lost souls, we are an extension of God's love story to them.

It just so happens, that because God loves us (our spirit), He has prepared a love justifiable for our flesh (marriage). This is no doubt, God's love manifested in a different form.

We'd know this if we recognized the God we serve. Often times we look to God, not for who He is, but what He has to offer. Therefore, we started off with that question at the beginning of the chapter for a reason.

How often are we seeking God just to know Him as God? How is it that our hearts can become so full of hidden agendas? I know that once we realize who God is, without trying to figure out what we can get out Him, we will find assurance.

Before the beginning was, God was and He is. In Job chapters 38-39, God asks Job some heavy questions about if Job was there when He was creating the earth. God asks Job if Job was the one that makes sure the waves only come so far before stopping in their wavy tracks? Paraphrasing, Job replies, 'how can I answer you? I'm sitting in awe attempting to comprehend just how excellent you are.' However, there is no way to comprehend how tremendous our God is.

It's been stated before that God is detailed orientated. He's thought of everything. From the beginning, He's known what the end game was going to be.

God's end game has always been about relationship. This is why it's been stressed so much in this book. God could have found contentment in knowing that He has the power to do anything, but He had a well thought out plan. He embarked on the greatest love journey.

God could have created the heavens and the earth simply for His enjoyment. However, God desired to share the beauty of His majesty with us, those He also created. He didn't just create us to show us this world, but most importantly to show His love.

Therefore, through Jesus, God has already accomplished a part of His plan in showing us His unconditional love. WE now need to take up our cross because WE are ambassadors for Christ.

But I pose a question; how can you be a representation of a God you don't know? Hmm…

There is a difference between knowing God and knowing of God. Often times we hear of acts that God has done for other people. We'll hear how He healed their bodies, saved their loved ones, provided when they didn't have a dime and so on down the line. This is knowing God through the lens of someone else. While we may be happy for them, we can never really appreciate God as a healer if we've never been sick. How do I know that God can provide if I've never lacked? How can you know God as a deliverer if you've never been addicted or burdened? Knowing who God truly is, is a part of our relationship with God in which He functions to increase our faith in Him.

However, God is yet God if He doesn't do a thing. Take a look around you; what do you see? Look up at the sky. Who put the clouds there? Who fixated the stars in the velvet abyss of outer space? Who causes the sun to radiate with heat, comfort and light, which never cease? How many times has your heart beat in this last minute? You don't know because you don't have control of it. You have taken for granted your very heartbeat because you've forgotten that it's God who's sustaining you.

God sustains the rhythm of your heart! It is far from your control. Often times we focus in on other things that don't deserve our attention, that we forget that our God is sovereign! He is amazing! He is awesome! He is wonderful! He is mighty! He is great! He is faithful! He is just! He is! WE forget, but He is God!

He is God! He is greater than every circumstance, disappointment, setback, setup, mishap, failure, every want and desire that you have ever had, have or will have. He is God!

God has all power and all authority. There is no place on this earth where He is not. How is it that we get so consumed in trying to play God for a fool that we forget He is all knowing? Prime example, we'll pretend that God is not aware of our secular extracurricular activities on Friday and Saturday night, when we attempt to engage in praise and worship on Sunday morning.

I know you wanted to hear how you could get a man? For those of you who were thinking that, I give you permission to close the book now, and bless a good friend with it. This book goes beyond finding a man. God is looking for a relationship with you. Do you know what that means? The creator of the heavens and the earth is seeking to have your heart!

Obviously you don't know what this means, for those still trying to figure out how they 'gone get a man.'

However, for those who recognize that it is not about simply walking down the aisle one day and pledging your life to another, but it's about the God who you will pledge your love before, the one who will bring you two together, have the audacity to keep reading, because God has greatness reserved for you.

To be receptive of the greatness God has in store for you, it starts with knowing God for yourself. According to Psalms 34:8 (KJV) "O taste and see that the Lord is good: blessed is the man that trusteth in him." This is personal. You have to know God for yourself. No longer should you be willing to live vicariously through other people's salvation. What if they backslide and you are completely unaware of their condition? They cannot be your guarantee into heaven.

I declare and decree that you, if you haven't already, have your own personal encounter with God. I'm speaking beyond Sunday morning church services. I decree that God manifest His presence in your life at home, work, school, the grocery stores, at the spa, and wherever you go. I pray that you begin to recognize God for who He is and not just for what He does.

In chapter two, we discussed the importance of having a personal encounter with God. We explored how God is infinite, gracious, merciful, faithful, compassionate and loving. Here we will explore a tad bit further by walking through some names of God.

Often times we don't see the diverse names of God in our King James Version of the Bible, which is evident that I use. Due to the poetic complexity of the Hebrew-Greek Bible (the languages in which the Bible was written) translation to English over simplified a great portion of the Bible to the point that we don't get the full emphatic meaning. Most of us don't know that there are names, which God was called in the Bible.

For example, Adonai (Adonoy): Usually used in conjunction with, or occurs with 'yehowah'. It is meant to express supreme authority, sovereignty, and God's matchlessness. God is matchless. Nothing and no one can be equated to God. Have you ever heard or told someone to get on your level? Well, no one can get on God's level. He is God all by Himself. His jurisdiction, power and dominance are the highest-ranking that there is. No position is greater than His.

God is Lord, Master, adonai. How has God exercised supreme authority in your life? How has God shown to be matchless?

Jehovah (Y'hovah): Which refers to God as being self-existent. In traditions of the past this name was not said out loud out of reverence for God. When we understand that God does not need us, it makes all the difference to understanding why His desire to have a relationship with us is amazing. God does not need my faith to be God, because He is self-existing. If I choose to never open my mouth in adoration or appreciation again, God will still be God.

Jehovah Jireh (Y'hovah yir'eh): We are familiar with this meaning, as Jehovah will provide. A self-existent God will provide. If a self-existent God provides, He must be self-sufficient. He has enough of His word to provide whatever it is that you need. All He has to do is open His mouth and speak. He is the source to your provision. If God can provide for everyone in this world, believe He has more than enough. He will not run out of provision. We always think of financial provisions or food. What about provisions for your health, your safety and your peace of mind? The quicker we realize who God is, the quicker God can manifest Himself in ways we could never imagine.

Meditate on this final thought. Jehovah is a name of God that speaks of Him being self-existent. From that, we were able to recognize that a self-existing God is self-sufficient. This doesn't simply imply that God doesn't need resources; it implies that He is the source! God has spoken everything and it was so. John 1:3 (KJV) "All things were made by him; and without him was not any thing made that was made." If you have ever read Genesis, the Bible clearly states that God "said," and what He had spoken came into existence, and when He saw it, He said that it was good. His resource is His word.

If God's resource is Himself, which is His word, there is no way possible that there is any lack in Him. God has given us the resources to everything we need! He's given us His word, and God's word is all that we need! While the Bible is the written word of God, I can also obtain sustenance directly from the source through relationship! This self-sustaining cycle proves that our God is matchless!

I thank Paul for detailing his walk by writing to the different churches and inadvertently speaking to me. However, when I have a relationship with God, I know God for myself! God will speak directly to me!

Why did I ask you to meditate on this? Right now as I am writing this, I'm single. Here is what's so crazy, but is yet so amazing. This time last year the desire to be married consumed me. It's all I really ever thought about. However, since then I've been on a journey to discover what it means to really know God intimately, I have such a peace in my mind that I can't explain. I'm enjoying Jesus!

In doing so, I have found myself smiling, laughing, and giggling as if I were in a relationship with my husband, also known as, Mr. Right-for-me. But no man has put this Kool-Aid smile on my face. I'm not in awe, intrigued or memorized by a man. This is all because of God. You know what? I feel safe knowing that me loving on God and feeling the way that I do, is not going to backfire on me. I can't go wrong loving God. Seeking His face is paying off tremendously. I find comfort in places I never thought to look. I pray and not just for myself but also for others; and to see the manifestation of God's power flowing through my life makes me love and seek Him the more.

Am I perfect? Absolutely not! There are days when I should be getting up to attend 6 a.m. prayer and turn the alarm off instead of hitting snooze. God is working on me, and I want to be who He's called me to be. I want and desire more of God. I yearn for His presence. So other days, I force myself to get up when I've only gotten a few hours of sleep.

My desire for God has nothing to do with getting married. Which is why, even though I have the desire to be married, it no longer consumes me. My reminders that I'm not married are: 1. writing this book, 2. talking to my friends who are married, 3. seeing couples in public, and 4. my daughter's constant reminder to me that she wants a little brother and sister. Being transparent, the fifth reminder would be the occasional handsome gentleman who caught me off guard with his deep, "hello." (Laughing hysterically).

Knowing God is principle. It's not a complicated process. The foundational question is do you want to know God for yourself? You have an amazing opportunity to do so! I'm not talking about getting to know President Barack Obama on a one-on-one basis; I'm speaking of Jehovah, Elohim, I AM, Immanuel. God is more than what you read in your Bibles; allow God to take residence in your life. Let the word of God come alive in you!

Beautiful women reading this book, it's no secret that God loves you! What God wants in return is for you to love Him for Him!

Before we delve a little deeper, let's be consistent and end this chapter with prayer.

God, master, Immanuel, Great I AM, we are calling on you now. You are God all by yourself. No one will ever compare to how great you are. God, we ask that you open the eyes of our understanding that we may come to know you in a way that you desire. Allow our understanding to be as complete as possible, because God, there is no way to fully know you in all your splendor, but God, if you could enlighten our current understanding of who you are, we'll learn to have a greater appreciation for you, our God! In Jesus name, Amen!

Chapter

8

The Restaurant

———✦———

In America, we can't help but be familiar with restaurants. There are different classes of restaurants depending on how much money you intend on spending.

We'll define a restaurant as a place with a hospitable environment where people pay to sit and dine. In the restaurant, the menu is the center stage, because what a restaurant serves is what attracts its patronage.

Restaurants have become so popular in American culture that we have fast-food restaurants, which are commonly under the umbrella of chain restaurants. Common ones we see within blocks of each other are Taco Bell, KFC, and Burger King.

Chain restaurants advertise their products by any means necessary, because they are vying for your business. They keep their prices affordable for reasons we will address soon enough. Because they are vying for your business, sometimes you don't realize why you're craving a burger. If you think about how many times you've seen a burger since the time you've gotten out of bed, you'd realize that the marketing team for fast food restaurants has played upon on your natural instinct to eat.

To eat is a natural process by which we acquire the nutrients needed to perform our daily tasks. Fast food can be delicious and easy on your pockets, but if you consider how it was prepared in order to look like the

81

advertisement, you'd realize that it doesn't provide the necessary nutrients to sustain you long-term. As a matter of fact, each fast food restaurant has a different owner because it's part of a franchise, which means they all have different standards.

Service and quality is not consistent across each restaurant within the franchise. Every owner has a different agenda. Some will cut corners in meal preparation or storage in an effort to keep their business running. Others will purchase low quality, hormone laden, and chemically modified meat in order to remain competitive by remaining affordable.

You realize that quality doesn't necessarily ensure a friendly and welcoming environment. A restaurant can serve some great food, but have poor service. A restaurant can have finger-licking good food, but the facility is not maintained, and the bathrooms are abominable. There are exceptions to the rule. You can find a hole-in-the-wall restaurant that looks scary on the outside, but the ambiance on the inside is shockingly fantastic. It's the world best kept secret because most people can't get past the exterior.

Why the details about restaurants? I'm glad you asked. In our parable, we've established who the Menu, the Owner and the consumer are. Now, let's consider the actual restaurant. The restaurant is a place where the owner can provide the consumer with substance that will satiate the consumers' desire. This is accomplished by having a menu! The restaurant provides a place in a favorable environment, where the consumer and the menu can be present at the same time. The Restaurant is analogous to the Holy Ghost or Holy Spirit.

What is the significance of the restaurant? Why didn't God set up a food stand? In our parable, God could have set up a food stand, but it's about experience. God doesn't want to appease your husband for a short period of time, but for a lifetime. It's about the encounter that you will have with Mr. Right-for-you and the emotion that will elicit. The Holy Spirit has great significance in this process.

What I love about our God is He doesn't operate a fast-food restaurant that specializes in expeditious, short-term satisfaction with no intent to satisfy a divinely sustained long-term hunger. The Holy Ghost brings the guarantee of quality and sufficiency. The Holy Ghost will make sure that what God has placed inside of you will provide the proper nourishment that your husband needs.

The Holy Ghost is the spirit of God. As we do, the Holy Spirit functions as a part to a whole. The Holy Ghost is a keeper, a comforter, an intercessor, and your reminder.

Jesus states in John 14:16 (KJV) "And I will pray the Father; and he shall give you another Comforter, that he may abide with you for ever;" Being a comforter encompasses a lot. Immediately our minds veers towards consolation when we think of someone being comforting. As a comforter, The Holy Spirit will not only console you, but also be an advocate and an aid. You are not in this alone! The next verse, verse 17 states "... but ye know him; for he dwelleth with you, and shall be in you."

The Holy Ghost is with you! As single women, we often go through cycles. Sometimes we're okay, and other times we feel lonely. We desire that companionship, and that closeness to share with a spouse. It is in your DNA to feel that way. There is nothing wrong with desiring to be married. However, when we assume that God is not in tune with how we are feeling, we are missing the fact that God has given us His spirit. God's Holy Spirit is a comforter that remains with us at all times. Why would Jesus send a comforter, if He weren't aware of your every state of being? He is very much aware of how you feel.

The Holy Spirit is not going to force Himself on you. You have to invite Him into every situation. It is hard to soothe, encourage, support, and help someone who doesn't want to be bothered. That is why it's oxymoronic for a Christian to feel lonely when our God is omnipresent. I'm not perfect and I've definitely felt lonely. Nevertheless, I've learned that when you call on God, He will move promptly and prove to be a very present help. Loneliness is small when you consider all that we confront on a daily basis for simply being women.

We will have temptations from now until kingdom come. Chocolate doesn't seem like such a bad temptation when eye candy has been starring at you all day long. I have a minor shoe obsession; your obsession may be handbags. A sale on shoes, therefore, is not going to cause you to get beside yourself and spend money you've been saving to pay off credit card debt. When I PMS I keep to myself; you may become a she-hulk. Regardless of what you confront on a daily basis, you can invite the Holy Spirit into each of them and He'll be a comforter, an advocate, and an aid.

We assume that some things are too small for God to be concerned with. We are God's children. Everything concerning you matters to Him. His love towards you won't allow Him to ignore you. Even if He tried, your spokesperson is constantly interceding on your behalf.

Let's revisit Romans 8: 26-27. From the NLT, starting at verse 27, and working our way backwards, vs. 27 "And the Father who knows all hearts knows what the Spirit is saying, for the Spirit pleads for us believers in harmony with God's own will." What would that sound like? Consider being in a backslidden condition. Maybe you've reverted back to old habits such as cursing, smoking, drinking or whatever, the Holy Spirit intercedes in such manner: 'The word spoken says he that has begun a good work shall perform it until the day of Jesus. You have begun a good work in your daughter. She desires to be close to you, but she's never been close to anyone. When she's felt alone in the past, she's done things to numb her pain. She's hurting now, merciful God. Please remain merciful and remember the sacrifice of your beloved son Jesus. Alcohol has been a comfort, but if you send me to remind her, I'll comfort her. She'll turn away from sin, and she'll love you because you've shown her your love. She'll draw close to you, if you allow me to whisper in her ear the instructions on how to draw nigh unto thee, our amazing king.' My God!

We have an advocate! The Holy Ghost is consistently interceding. He is fighting for us, pleading on our behalf, so that we can hear "well done, thy good and faithful servant." That's powerful. Think about it. We thank God all the time for not giving up on us when we think He should have. The truth, He would have hadn't it not been for the Holy Spirit pleading with Him to remember why He sent Jesus. All that His only begotten son went through would have been in vain if God withdrew His grace and mercy from our lives. I'm humbled to have such an advocate that I don't deserve!

Verse 26, (NLT), "And the Holy Spirit helps us in our weakness. For example, we don't know what God wants us to pray for. But the Holy Spirit prays for us with groanings that cannot be expressed in words." Often times we have intentions to do the right thing, however, secretly we are fighting internal battles. Lust may not be your internal battle, but self-pity is. They are internal battles that we either are reluctant to address, or it hurts to address. We fear the light of God will illuminate and also project the darkness within our lives. As we internalize these feelings we don't know how to pray about what we're struggling with. Again, sometimes we feel there are some things that God doesn't want to be bothered with. Therefore, the Holy Spirit groans with us in a language that God understands. He's not advocating for us only when we sin, but also when we are seeking to be delivered! You can be in a good place and doing well, the Holy Spirit is still there praying.

I declare healing now! Someone reading this book didn't realize that the spirit of God is working on your behalf in such a magnificent way. Believe it. You are not in this alone! The next time you feel alone, bind that devil from your mind and let him know with authority that God's got you!

We all needed to be reminded that even what we don't say is said. Even when we can't pray, the spirit, The Holy Spirit is praying. That's powerful.

The Holy Spirit is also our reminder. According to John 14:26 (KJV) "But the Comforter, which is the Holy Ghost, whom the Father will send in my name, he shall teach you all things, and bring all things to your remembrance, whatsoever I have said unto you." It should be more and more evident that God has provided all that we need to be all that He desires.

He didn't put us here to fail. The Holy Spirit is with us to aid us in all things. We get so caught up in life circumstances that we forget just how good our God is. He didn't send His Son Jesus, draw us, save us, deliver us, and fill us with His Spirit for us to fail. Where is the logic in that? Consequently, when we face our Goliaths and our Jericho walls, we are so quick to think defeat. The Holy Ghost has to remind us what the word of God says. He has to remind you of the promises of God. He has to prompt you to re-read through God's track record. He doesn't just remind us of God's goodness, but the promises God has spoken to us. Sometimes He has to even remind us of the calling on our lives when we become self-driven.

Not only will The Holy Ghost remind you, but also He will teach you. The Holy Spirit will use the word of God in everyday life experiences to teach you how to be what God desires. Who better else since He understands what the will of God is.

I can attest to this; when the enemy is creating chaos in your work environment and he's attempting to elicit an ungodly response out of you, the Holy Ghost will tell you to keep your mouth shut. You'll begin to develop an itch; an itch is to let them, those being used by the enemy, have a small piece of your mind. The Holy Ghost keeps telling you to shut your mouth and walk away. That's hard when your character is being attacked.

It's hard when you hear that someone is lying on you, and they pretend that everything is great and continue to smile in your face. You have every desire to swipe that smile away, but it's the Holy Ghost that reminds you of the power in the name of Jesus. It's the Holy Ghost that restrains you!

To restrain means to prevent someone from displaying or giving away to strong urges or emotions. The Holy Ghost will only keep you if you want to be kept! If you want to be kept, God will seal you with His spirit. Ephesians 1:13, (KJV) "In whom ye also trusted, after that ye heard the word of truth, the gospel of your salvation: in whom also after that ye believed, ye were sealed with that holy Spirit of promise." The sealing of the Holy Spirit is a security deposit. It insures what God is investing in you, to ensure it remains in you, and that is why the Spirit restrains and constrains you! This is why the Holy Ghost is called a keeper.

This foundational review of the Holy Spirit is important in order for us to move forward. We have to understand how He functions in our lives to comprehend why metaphorically speaking He is the restaurant.

The Holy Ghost is not only the restaurant but He is everything that comes with the restaurant.

We've discussed in detail how we have to prepare according to the standards of God when Mr. Right-for-us comes looking. We don't want him to survive off of chips and salsa while he's waiting, because we know those are only temporary fixes. What about Mr. Right-for-you? What if he isn't prepared to dine?

I love the Holy Ghost because if you yield yourself over to the divine authority of God, He will make sure that no one makes it past the entrance. Some restaurants have certain stipulations for you to even enter the facility. Have you ever seen a sign that reads, "no shoes no service," or "shirt required?" Well, some restaurants don't allow jeans or tennis shoes because they enforce a strict dress code.

The Holy Spirit enforces a strict dress code. Some men will not even have the luxury of even walking through the door because they do not meet the dress requirements. What are these dress requirements?

They are the basic things that we seem to overlook when checking out Mr. TALLDARKANDHANDSOME; is he saved? Since you are a Christian woman reading this book, I sure hope you are expecting to marry a man who loves God! Not only does he love God, but also has a relationship with God.

Amos 3:3, KJV, "Can two walk together, except they be agreed?" If you are to continue on this journey and get married, it would be nice to marry someone who is going in the same direction, wants the same things out of life as you do, and someone who is matched or superior in ambition and drive. If you marry someone who isn't saved, you are more likely to be unhappy let alone constantly disappointed. Marrying someone with a different belief system is even more fatal to your spiritual walk.

If God is attempting to elevate you spiritually and an uncompromising, unsaved husband is your hindrance because he doesn't understand why the church needs more of your time in addition to Wednesday and Sunday's, you'll always be in a tug-a-war between your marriage and your relationship with God. No marriage that God has ordained will ever be in competition with Him! God will not bless you with anything that contradicts who He is. Remember God is the perfect matchmaker, and the Holy Spirit will check inappropriately dressed men at the door!

Why would you want to argue constantly with your husband if you don't have to? When you marry someone with different beliefs than those of your own, be prepared for battle. If God has your heart, why would you want to give it over to idols or false gods? That is exactly what a husband who doesn't share your beliefs will attempt to do. He will coerce you into his beliefs because it would make life easier on him. Why do you think God told Israel over and over again not to mingle with heathen nations? Instead of Israel being God's chosen people they would have become a mixed breed, adopting the ideology of the surrounding nations. This is why the woman at the well mentioned that Jews didn't have any dealings with the Samaritans, because Samaritans were a crucible of religions and cultures.

Simply put, if he isn't saved, the Holy Ghost will deny him entry. Some men have had a desire to approach you, but won't because they don't meet certain standards. It should feel good to know that the Holy Spirit has your best interest at heart.

Realize that men who aren't saved are passerby's; he's there to spectate or dine for free. We can go into detail when we discuss the dating game. Since he's simply passing by, don't lose heart if he's cute, educated, established and polished on the outside. He needs to be able to appeal to what is on the inside of you.

If a man is saved, the Holy Ghost will begin to look for evidence of Himself within that man. A man can be saved, but has he been delivered? If God doesn't want to present you to your husband as a mess, what makes you think God wants to present you to a mess? He can be saved on yesterday, but that doesn't mean he is delivered. Some things come out strictly by fasting and prayer because they are strong holds.

This is going to sound contradictory to what I just said, however, in rare cases I believe that God allows some people to marry women and men who are not delivered because the husband or wife helps to administer healing to that individual. This is why the leading of the Holy Spirit is so important.

Being honest, I don't want to marry someone who is struggling with sexual addictions. I want him delivered if that was his issue. Why? I don't want to ever wonder if what we do in the confines of our bedroom is ever enough to gratify his appetite. If it's not and he isn't used to exercising self-control with me, then when a foolish woman throws herself at my husband he's not going to be able to control himself with her either. Side bar, there is nothing wrong with a husband who has a sexual appetite, or libido. It has purpose!

Is he delivered? If he's not, he's not appropriately dressed to dine! There are some things you should want your man to be delivered from before you even meet. Why? You shouldn't want to be tempted. I don't want Mr. Right-for-me's baggage to bring temptation into my life. I have enough as a single woman to resist, I don't need any extra! If he curses now, but by the time we get married he'll be delivered isn't good enough. How can he both bless God and curse me at the same time! Why would I want to even pick up that habit again? Before he can enter he needs to be delivered!

Throughout this book, as God is giving me the words to write, I've seen both where I overrode the Holy Spirit, and also saw Him keeping unqualified individuals at bay. He's always been looking out for me because He knows what God has in store for me. All I ever have had to do was trust that.

I encourage you before continuing, to look back over your life. Literally take the time to examine the choices that you've made when it comes to men. Now that you are saved, sanctified, Holy Ghost filled and fire baptized, what patterns of behavior in men do you still allow to slip through the cracks or do you stop unqualified diners immediately?

What I love about the Holy Spirit is that we as women can truly relax during this process. If we were to completely yield over to the divine will of God, the Holy Spirit will mediate the process of bringing the right one our way. One definition of mediate I looked up was, to form a connecting link between. I really like that! A restaurant brings the person with an appetite to a place where it can be satisfied.

The Holy Spirit forms the linkage, the bond between men who are longing for a wife, and women who are longing for a husband. We as women can be patient in our wait knowing that the Holy Spirit will dictate when the man is ready to come in and dine. With all the taste testing you've been through, you should want someone who is worthy enough to enjoy what you have to offer.

'That's too spiritual!' May I remind you that we are spiritual beings, and if as a Christian woman this is too spiritual for you, and this parable doesn't seem practical, by all means enter your prayer closet and ask God what you need to do for you to get a man. However, realize that God wants your heart first, and that is the basics of this book.

Back to the scheduled programming; anyone can walk in a restaurant dressed as suave and smooth as the law allows, but if he doesn't have enough money to match his appetite, he's come in vain. In the natural, if you walk into Red Lobster with an appetite for steak, lobster, an extra side, plus an appetizer, and a virgin Peña Colada, you'd better have the coins for that meal. Red Lobster is fairly reasonable compared to someone who orders the same meal at Ruth Chris.

Likewise spiritually, if the man makes it past the door he needs to be able to afford you. I'm not talking about your mall bill or living expenses. If you recall earlier in the book I mentioned someone I dated didn't have the capacity to love me the way I deserved? I felt inadequate and unappreciated in my attempts to love him. Read carefully ladies; a man who cannot afford you emotionally and spiritually can bring about as much disaster as a man who isn't saved.

Brother man can be saved, handsome, employed, debt-free and celibate all he wants, but if he doesn't have the ability and the power to love you, appreciate you, encourage you, support you, pray for you and to the protect the gift and virtue that you possess as a woman, he is not it!

It's not uncommon to go into a restaurant and see what they offer before deciding if you want to eat there. In modern society all one has to do is pull up a search engine on their smart phone and look for an online menu. Our God operates uniquely. Capacitance is evident to the Maître D' from the moment a consumer looks through the menu. Often times if the consumer looks unsatisfied or uneasy with what's on the menu, they'll offer a suggestion based on the consumer desires. Sometimes those suggestions are for either the consumer to choose a more affordable restaurant, or a restaurant designed for an exquisite or highly sensitive palate.

You are a beautiful woman, but not every woman reading this book can handle being a ministers or pastors wife. Not every woman reading this book can handle her husband constantly prophesying to both men and women during extended and extensive ecclesiastical assignments.

Yes, some men will leave the restaurant because they don't have the capacity for you, however, some will leave because although you are a great, blessed, gifted and beautiful woman, you can't satisfy their desire. You may be a praying woman and he definitely needs that, but he really needs a wife that is so full of faith that not only is she interceding on the behalf of others, but also her ministry is laying hands on the sick and they recover. Some things he really needs are not even ministry related.

You may be comfortable living a simple quiet life. You don't want the headaches of home ownership so you're comfortable renting your entire life. You may have a desire to change careers, however, you like the security of having a paycheck every two weeks so you never even start working on a resume to prepare to advance. Your complacency may look like laziness or lack of ambition to someone who comes in to dine. He can't imagine not owning at least two homes, in which one creates wealth for retirement and your posterity. He may be an entrepreneur and he's always finding ways to invest, or market his skills to create and expand his brand. You two are socially and economically incompatible.

God is awesome! He has created for you a husband who is 100% compatible with you. Will it always feel like it or look like it? Answer this question; have you ever had a dress or pair of jeans that fit just right? Maybe you gained weight and they didn't fit the same? You were determined to get back in that dress or those jeans by any means necessary, because you loved the fit and how you looked. You didn't love that dress or that pair of jeans any less when you gained weight. You did the work to get back in them.

You and your husband will be 100% compatible, but you two will also differ in opinions occasionally. That's okay, but I'm sure because you'll love each other, that you won't allow a difference in opinion to hinder your happily ever after.

The Maître D', the Holy Ghost, will make suggestions to the consumer. There is nothing wrong with that. There is one man that is just right for you and you for him. I'd rather know that I'm with a man God has predestined for me to be with, than be with a man who will resent me or I resent him.

Therefore, not only does Mr. Suave have to have the coins to dine, but he needs the appetite too. The Holy Ghost will mediate it all if you allow Him to. He has both your best interest at heart and Mr. Sauvé's best interest at heart. All we have to do is trust the process.

Before we end this chapter understand that although we use these analogies to get a better understanding to the mystery of getting married, realize it's deeper than that.

We have discussed so much, and it's all in vain if we don't recognize that God is in control of the entire process. It makes sense if He's the only one who knows who your husband is. Some of us have control issues, making it harder for us to succumb to the will of God, but it is possible. It's possible through relationship.

Often time we don't trust the process because we don't trust God. We don't trust God because we don't know who God is. Hmm? Didn't we talk about that earlier? We did! This is all coming full circle. Wow, how could that possibly be?

For some women, it never seemed like this long drawn out process that you are reading in this book. Some women, when they fell in love with God they fell hard. They were so madly in love with God, that it seemed like Mr. Right-for-them came out of nowhere. Their courtship was short and maybe they were engaged or even married within months of meeting or dating each other.

The truth ladies, it's not a long process unless you want it to be. It definitely won't seem like a process when it's done right. Why? If you are in love with God, and are relaxed in Him, the Holy Ghost will mediate everything and before you know it, Mr. Right-for-you will be kneeling on one knee asking for your hand in marriage.

I think God gave me this dream specifically for this book, but years ago, about two years to be more precise; I had a dream that I was at the altar getting married. My groom was as handsome as a man could be. The entire time I was in shock because I couldn't believe that I was finally getting married. After the ceremony, there was an influx of people, predominately women, asking me how it felt to be married. All I could say was, "I didn't know I was getting married today." None of them looked at me like I was crazy because honestly, I think I was simply hearing my thoughts, not what I was actually telling them.

It will happen! When it does beautiful women, it will be so quick that it takes you by surprise. All you have to do is relax in God, and truly love Him first. Allow the Holy Spirit to bring you two together. Besides He's here to do the hard part. We just have to allow the divine will of God to unfold as He foresaw it.

Dear God, we thank you for the Holy Spirit. Thank you Jesus for sending the comforter. We appreciate you Holy Spirit for your labor of love. Thank you for interceding on our behalf. Thank you for keeping us fresh in the mind and heart of God. Thank you for looking past our many faults and deficiencies and seeing our need; our need to experience true unconditional love and forgiveness. Thank you for leading and guiding us. Forgive us for the many times when we pushed back your gentle hand. Thank you for the teaching, for the constraining, and for wrestling with our stubborn will. We surrender all to you, because you truly know what is best for us. In Jesus name, Amen!

Chapter

9

The Dating Game

———

I've never been the dating type. It's not that I don't like to go on dates. I think they're fun. However, no matter how fun they are, dating is a lot of work. I've come to this resolve; I've always kept myself busy and maintained a barrier to avoid dating. Of course I've been approached, and yes I've dated, but for all the work I've invested into dating, I'm still single. That is frustrating to me. Therefore, I don't date. I want a sure return.

There is also my fear of dating. Now I know I'm not the only one in this boat, but it seems like when I decide to date, I'm a magnet. You would think I was a neon sign reading, 'ask me out,' or 'flirt with me and see if I flirt back.' I get an influx of attention from some qualified and some highly unqualified individuals, and I feel flattered. Okay, I watered that down, I feel absolutely amazing; my head grows five times its normal confident size; which is already quite large. My fear is that I'll get beside myself and date multiple people, and that eventually somewhere in my dating frenzy, each gentleman proposes around the same time and I'm left with a mess. Attention can make you think some strange things.

That is only part of my fear of dating. I've come a long way in a short amount of time to get back into the eyesight and earshot of God. I've established a real relationship and I'm working day by day to make it stronger and better. I don't want to turn my attention from God and focus it on dating to the point that I forget where God has brought me from, and I fall into a lifestyle that is contrary to holiness.

I've been saved since I was fifteen, however, I backslid in college. I was in a backslidden condition much longer than I should have been because my attention wasn't on God. I allowed one relationship to consume me to the point that I allowed cycles of hurt to handicap me for years. When the relationship was good, it was great. But when it was bad I took it, thinking it would get better after a while. It was like being addicted to a drug, I was always looking for the high, the euphoria of it all.

I'm not going to blame my upbringing for my ignorance; however, when you've never seen examples of true love, or how a man should treat his woman, then you go through life trying to figure out what it's supposed to look and feel like. I realized before I decided to call it quits that I deserved better whether I was backslider or not.

To choose me over a bad relationship, I had to realize who I was and my value. So I began building myself up in the word of God. I became as active in ministry as I could, including be involved in my church singles ministry.

On the road to recovery and discovery, the enemy recognized that I was maturing and valuing who God created me to be. God allowed my father to pass, and in that season of my life, I had met someone else. Before we went on our first date, God specifically told me to walk away. My thoughts were how could I when this person had been so supportive of me during my time of bereavement?

I deliberately disobeyed God, by not discerning what God was trying to keep me from. Now one of my highest spiritual gifts is the spirit of discernment. But at that time, because I was emotionally compromised, I didn't have enough sense to pray and ask God to show me this individual's spirit. I figured since this man was a preacher, could pray, knew the word and was so supportive that I would be safe giving it a try.

I remember the day that God showed me the individual in the spirit because of something he had said. God told me again to walk away. At that point, I recognized exactly where a relationship with that person would go. I was going to walk away at that point, but I made a dangerous mistake; I thought that if I allowed my light to shine, this person would realize that I was a true Christian, and I held tight to my convictions in living a life that was pleasing to God.

In less than a year, I never thought that I would experience the same kind of hurt again. I never considered what not walking away would have cost me. Due to my disobedience, I was hurt and disappointed. That last relationship was how this book was birthed. A real father will get tired of his children repeating the same mistakes, and he'll eventually intervene to give them a chance to grow.

This is God intervening. You too may have been the victim of someone else's games. You may have had your heart broken because a man you thought was a complete gentleman had ulterior motives the moment he laid eyes on you. He was simply a spectator or passerby observing you to figure out what he can get out of you at no cost. He never had any real intentions to come in and sit down and enjoy all of you for the person God created you to be. For one reason he could not was because you were not his.

What saddens me about today's society is that there are those men who don't really understand or appreciate the value that there is in a woman. So they don't exemplify kingly attributes, and they run through women wondering why so many of us are hurting and bitter. What makes this trend worse, is some of us women consistently put ourselves out there to be victims while saying we're waiting for God to reveal the right one.

Often times we override the leading of God and attempt to take on the task of dating and getting married into our own hands and become wounded in the process. I'm not saying that every relationship you've been in and got hurt as a result was your fault. However, when God tells you to "walk away," and you attempt to mold that relationship into something that it was never meant to be, don't be surprised when it backfires. It is apparent that Christians are getting caught with the modern mentality of dating.

We're living in a time where most people do not share the same values and even religion as their grandparents. Let's be honest and get straight to the point; dating in today's society is an all-inclusive test drive. Men and women are not waiting until the honeymoon to experience fireworks; those happen within weeks of meeting each other. As a matter of fact so does cohabitation. Why the rush? Could it be that even in today's Christian society, we're desperate to have what we want, all the time, especially with no objections or rejection from God?

In this modern era, I've noticed that some people are not looking for commitment, but they're looking for convenience. They want a facsimile of a loving relationship, however, they don't want the dedication, or to invest the time into building something that's not only worth their time, but also their attention.

I'm the polar opposite. All godly women should be for that matter. I yearn for the commitment and the loving relationship and I'm willing to put in the work. Because of my past, I'm determined that for me to put in the work, he has to be the right man for me. I've come to realize that my fear is not dating itself. My real fear is that I will override God again, and invest the time and the effort and get the ring, but never make it down the aisle.

Apparently I am a part of the microwave generation that perpetuates the modern mentality of dating. Everything has to be quick because we don't want to work for what we want. To be honest I don't completely disagree, because that is how most of my generation was raised. We were taught to dream big and shoot high, but never given the tools to show us how properly. Therefore, we've created shortcuts for virtually everything. If I could get married next week, I would; but I also differ from most in my generation. I grew up having to always work for what I wanted. I could never find the shortcuts. Therefore, I realize that in order to build something that guarantees 'until death do you apart,' I have to put in every bit of effort to make it just that. Whether you're a part of my generation or not, you may have fallen victim or been the villain of the mentality that created "The Dating Game."

The basics of The Dating Game, are to get out of someone what you want for a limited time to avoid attachment. Silly right? But do you realize how many people have actually been engaged, but never walked down the aisle? The engagement was a pacifier, meant to keep one party happy while the other continued to drain what they wanted. You would think everyone looking for real love from a long-term relationship wouldn't waste time pacifying one person, when they could simply wait on the right person. However, from both genders of various age groups and ethnic backgrounds, people are purposefully avoiding love.

If you are constantly unavailable because you have a tendency to date often, or more than one person at a time, you're not really waiting to be with that one. You are playing the dating game, and even if it doesn't feel intentional, you're avoiding real love.

Before any of you chastise me, I don't think there is anything wrong with a man taking you out to dinner or to the movies. It is good to have friends of the opposite sex that you can have fun with for funs sake. If you are dating, however, you need to make sure his intentions are clear as well as those of your own.

To be even more simple, by the end of your first date he should know that you are celibate and that your intentions are to wait on God to bring the right man in your life. The man you're dating may be it, and then again, he might not be. If a man is going to take you out, you as a woman should want clarity in knowing what his intentions are. You do that first by acknowledging God.

I personally don't want a man who has to beat around the bush. Yes, God is working on me, however, if I have to pry out of you why you decided to ask me out, I don't need to be out with you. It seems harsh, but you have to guard yourself especially your heart. Some men have ulterior motives. How can you discern that if your spiritual guard is not up?

Proverbs 4:23a (KJV) "Keep thy heart with all diligence." We're going to work on this first part of the scripture in relation to this last paragraph. There are a few definitions that I found for keep, but one that I really liked said to retain or to reserve for future use. Diligence is careful and persistent work or effort. This scripture says, reserve your heart for future use, by being careful and persistently putting forth an effort. If you as a Christian woman are not careful with your heart, which you should have already given to God, then you become prone to heartbreak.

Taking our scenario for example, let's assume you asked the gentleman you were on a date with what his intentions were with you. To be honest, this shouldn't intimidate any man whose intentions are sincere and pure. If he says he wants to get to know you better, okay, that's fine. You now know, that one, you don't need to be fantasying about what your children would look like. Often time we get so caught up in "what if he's the one," that we begin taking innocent relationships to a whole different level in our minds. That is not guarding your heart. He might actually just want to get to know as a person. You two may become good friends or business partners, and not married lovers, and that's okay. Then again, you never know; it may blossom into something beyond friendship, but you have to allow the Holy Spirit to do the footwork.

Be that as it may, if he tells you he is interested in getting to know you as a person, don't you as a woman attempt to manipulate his heart or his mind. Some of us women have or have had ulterior motives. Instead of being a victim, we're the villains in this game. It is apparent that some women believe that every man wants them, and they therefore exercise deception on men who simply are interested in friendship.

Why expel all that energy, desperately wanting a man to like you erotically? I've always wondered, in this scenario, does the woman even like the man like that, or does she just want every man drooling over her? To be honest, I love attention, but that kind of attention is trouble. If every man is drooling over me, it means I appeal to his flesh, not to his ego or his intellect. When I say ego, I'm not using it in a derogatory manner. If I appeal to his flesh, I don't boost or contribute to his increased self-worth or perception, which means I absolutely do not entreat or challenge his intellect. A small disclaimer, it's not that men don't like to feel challenged, it's that they don't like the feeling of not being needed.

Therefore, if I'm expelling all my energy to simply appeal to his flesh, I'm only looking for one thing, sex. I've been there and done that. If I can only make a man feel good sensually, he does not have the capacity for me emotionally and intellectually. If I'm only looking for my senses to be tantalized, then I myself don't have the capacity for anything other than a short-lived orgasm. Amen, somebody!

Yes, we're starting to get into some real deep stuff. However, there is no way we can go forward and some of us are wearing our pain like a uniform, and others are manipulator's; both of which who says she desires God's best.

There are some of us who instead of being played you are the player. You play the dating game well, but it's time to put away the games and get real with God. If you don't want a committed relationship, then do you! Why is that so hard? Oh, that's right, you're not used to being by yourself.

We'll talk about that later. Getting back to our scenario. If the gentleman you're on a date with tells you that he likes you and is interested in seeing where this might go, he is already unsure. He was honest, but if he likes you and knows what he wants out of life, there has to be something in him liking you, that fits the vision he has for his life. This is my personal opinion, but if I were on this date I would assume from that point that he wasn't it. Again that seems harsh, but when you've had your heart broken, you know what questions to ask and will be able to discern when a man is sincere. However, first you need healing from past relationships so it's not a self-sabotaging behavior.

Realize certain behaviors have certain actions. A man who is unsure why he wants to date you is more than likely unsure what benefit you would be to his future. Think about it this way, and I pray you catch the revelation, but once God has revealed you to Mr. Right-for-you, he will be watching you. You're completely unaware that you're captivating him. So before he ever asks you out, he would have already prayed to God to provide the right opportunity for him to entreat you as his future queen.

On that note, getting back to our scenario, as women sometimes we think with our hearts, and we hear something completely different than what was said. We might have heard, 'he likes me and he's interested.' Again, we begin to build an illusion and we run with it. This is not guarding our hearts. Next month this man might meet his future wife, and has less time to get to know you as a friend. Don't act like you wouldn't become all twisted in the face because you heard what you wanted to hear. Keep your hearts, and reserve them for the right man. As a matter of fact, God made the first reservation! His reservation is secure. He will keep your heart protected and God is waiting to hand it over to a man that is worthy.

Why should we guard our hearts diligently? The Bible in Proverbs 4:23b (KJV) states "for out of it are the issues of life." Out of the heart flow the issues of life. Whether you want to speak literally or figuratively they would both boil down to what God is trying to say. Let's take both the literal and figurative together. The wisdom given in Proverbs suggests that we need to guard our hearts or our minds, because out of them pours the issues of life.

Using our scenario for example, there is no reason to get bent out of shape if a man tells you he is interested in getting to know you as a person and that's all he has been doing the last six months. Being bent out of shape, tells God that you allowed your heart or the illusions in your mind to take control of your actions and not your dedication and trust in God. Often times as women involved in the dating game, we drop one man quick, and we then move quickly to the next. However, even if you didn't attach yourself physically to that man, you have mentally.

You've been playing out thousands of scenarios over a six-month period, so actually you've attached yourself spiritually to that man. Therefore, with this next beau you're bitter for no reason. This new fella may really be interested in you, but your aura reads damaged! Your life is screaming broken! Why does he see you as damaged? All that is flowing from you are broken thoughts, broken promises, insecurities, because of what you think the last man did to you. But you put your heart in that fantasy, not God. As a matter of fact, you're so consumed in your feelings that you haven't realized that this new guy has bounced. Sure he might physically be sticking around, but he has mentally checked out, and he's looking for someone a little bit- well- more stable. Now as a woman who calls herself a child of God, you attempt to heal in order to repeat the same sad cycle all over again. Are you ever going to get tired of it?

Guard your heart! Out of your heart flow the issues of your life! Whatever has captivated your thoughts has your heart. Whatever has your heart has enslaved your mind, which inevitably enslaves you. We were once slaves to sin, and with that sin came a lot of emotional baggage. Could it be that you never let some of that emotional baggage go, so you find ways to incorporate it in any and every area of your life? That is exactly what self-sabotaging behavior is.

We are to keep our hearts and our minds to avoid enslavement of our minds to things that are not fruitful. If something is not fruitful it's detrimental because it doesn't produce life. If it doesn't produce life, death is near! Why then are some of us constantly in and out of unfruitful relationships pretending that we are waiting for the right one?

You don't want commitment you want convenience. You like the thought of having somebody, but you aren't really waiting to spend your life with somebody. Your mouth tells your friends that you want to be married, but your actions tell God a completely different story. You complain that all men are "dogs," but every time one asks you out, you say yes instead of no.

If you have been delivered don't return to bondage. When you say you're a child of God and that you are saving yourself, specify whether that is for marriage or not, because when you're giving it up, expect the enemy to tempt you often. Let your no, be a solid NO!

Some of us that are single, God can't bless in this season in our lives because we are being foolish. I'm not condemning anyone. We've all sinned and come short of God's glory. I have a question, what do you really want woman of God? If you find yourself being drawn away by your lust, what do you want? How can you get close to God and embrace what He has for you?

Some of us are dating without cause. We're like nomads, except we wander from relationship to unfruitful relationship. Our minds are not set on permanence. We aren't interested in settling and multiplying. We don't want the luxury of actually being married; we just want the benefits. Thus, we attempt to find it in many different men instead of one created perfectly for us.

What song is your heart singing to God? What issues are flowing out of your heart? What is your life telling God? Are you unavailable? Do you want to be married?

If you haven't guarded your heart, you've more than likely been the victim of someone else's games, or burned by the ones you've played. Me personally, I don't like people playing with my heart or my emotions, so I've learned to guard it. Although I am consumed with loving on God, when the time comes I want the right man to have my heart. He'll know how to guard it and protect it. There will be no foolishness when the right man comes into my life. I'm not expecting him to be perfect or bionic, but he will be mine. God will bless me with that specific man for a reason.

Earlier in this chapter I mentioned how Mr. Right-for-you will study you. That's real. Every person attempting to accomplish anything and be successful has a plan. While as a woman you are not a trophy, you will bring a sense of accomplishment to your husband. Think about it, you've heard men say how blessed they are to have a wife they don't deserve. For him to marry an amazing woman be believes should be marrying presidents, princes, senators, models, actors and the works, but she marries him, that is a sense of accomplishment. He will study you, because he's determined to marry you. Therefore, he is figuring out how to approach you.

The point that I really want to make here is that Mr. Right-for-you is sure. If you were to ask him why he asked you out, he will be able to tell you without hesitation or remorse. Sometimes it may start with getting to know the woman behind the smile, but eventually, when it's the right one, he will be interested in sealing a bond through marriage.

When he's the right one, he'll realize that getting to know the woman behind the smile is recognizing that when you smile like you do, he feels comfort and love. When you date the right man, he's not just intrigued that you can hold a conversation on multiple fronts. He's fascinated that a woman who wears so many hats already, has enough time to involve herself in her church, her community, career, and family and still have stability. When Mr. Right-for-you sees that you wait for him to open your door or to pull out your chair, he won't assume that you're high-maintenance. He will recognize that you are a woman who deserves the respect of a man and will treat you with respect. However, if you keep lending your time and expelling all your energy into dating the wrong men, you'll never get to this point.

I encourage you all to evaluate where you are. If you find yourself always in a relationship, but each one has been just as unfruitful as the last, don't pronounce death in your future my continuing in the same cycle. Spend some time to focus on you. It's okay to be single. It is only a stigma if you make it one. Speak honestly to yourself; what is so wrong with being single?

Learn to guard your heart and your mind from harmful thinking. Be sure of what you want from life and pursue it. God will bring the right man in your life where no illusions are needed. Most importantly stay in the will of God.

Again, there is nothing wrong with friends going out to have fun, but that tone needs to be set from the beginning. You shouldn't be afraid or hesitant in telling any man who approaches you that you are celibate and waiting for God. You should be able to say 'I'm interested in being your friend until God tells me otherwise.' If you are unsure if God has brought this man into your life, don't be afraid to pray and ask God for clarity and direction. If this is hard you need to check your relationship with God and work on that first!

Understand that as our father, God doesn't want to see us hurting constantly from being disappointed, lied to, and walked out on from relationship after relationship. He doesn't want us to take on a mentality to consequently be a user of men either. He truly desires to see us happy and complete in Him. If you constantly find yourself disappointed because of the men you've dated and said "I give up," then maybe it's time to allow God to heal you, and wait for Him to bring the right man your way.

Dear God, we need you! God draw us closer to you and help us to see ourselves as you see us. God show us every weight that keeps us off track and out of your divine will, and then illuminate the right path for us to take. Help us to realize that dating is not a hobby. Help us to focus on what is important, and to keep our hearts and minds guarded. We thank you that in the right season, the right man will come and we will be blessed. Until then, prepare us for the promise. In Jesus name, Amen!

Chapter

10

Anticipate!

—✦—

*O*riginally, the name of this chapter was going to be 'The Wait.' But two things happened before I was able to write this chapter, 1. A book came out with the same title and I like being original, and 2. I wanted to end this book with a bang. For the purpose of this chapter, Anticipate has a lot more life than The Wait. In reality, we'd rather say we anticipated a blessing before we say we waited for a blessing. There is nothing wrong with waiting. As a matter of fact to anticipate is to wait, but there something about anticipating that makes the wait different.

To wait is a lack of progression, movement, and action while expecting something to happen or come to pass. To wait is to be passive. On the other hand, anticipation is actively waiting by preparation. If you anticipate the rain, you will carry an umbrella. If you are waiting for the rain, you only get your umbrella once it starts raining.

When you anticipate, you have faith enough to believe that it will happen! It doesn't matter when it happens, the fact that you know it will happen, prompts you to place yourself in a position for reception. This kind of active faith, for we know that faith without works is dead, moves God to action.

If you are waiting for God to send the rain, but you haven't prepared for it, are you really expecting it to rain? That doesn't demonstrate faith in the God you serve, and the God that you have established a relationship with.

Faith is a requirement. However, you need to make sure you're operating in your faith and not your nerves. Anticipation is not the same thing as anxiety. In other words, if I anticipate something, I'm not anxious about it. To be anxious shows a complete lack of faith. If I am anxious I am uncertain.

The bible tells us in Philippians 4:6-7 (KJV) vs 6 "Be careful for nothing, but in every thing by prayer and supplication with thanksgiving let your request be made known unto God." vs 7 " And the peace of God, which passeth all understanding, shall keep your hearts and minds through Christ Jesus."

Before we incorporate this scripture, realize that there is nothing wrong with anticipating the arrival of your future husband. I encourage you to get excited about one day meeting a man that you will spend the rest of your life with. Know that he'll be all that you could ever hope for and then some.

No matter what we are having faith enough to believe God for, we are to be careful for nothing. On version states we are to be anxious for nothing. What does this mean? There is no reason for us to be uncertain. To do that, it clearly states that we first must remain prayerful. You have to maintain open communication with God. Often times when we're anxious, we're also failing to pray. How can God talk to you, encourage and prepare you for marriage if you don't open that line of communication with Him? We get so caught up in when, when God is trying to show us how, but we won't spend the time to listen. If you ask someone a question, don't you want to hear his or her response? Shouldn't you listen for instructions?

Supplication is closely related to prayer, but it omits the element of worship and appreciation toward God. It is simply a humble request. God doesn't have to grant us anything. He is the creator of all things. When we approach our King, we ought to have enough respect for Him to do it humbly. You don't demand God to do anything. You ask Him. The word says when you ask God for anything ask with thanksgiving!

What is thanksgiving? Gratitude! As stated previously, God doesn't have to do anything, but the fact that He even hears our prayer and supplications should make us grateful. I desire to be married, and I'm thankful that God has created a husband specifically for me. Even if I don't meet Mr. Right-for-me in two or three years, I'm thankful that God is preparing us for a lifetime of friendship and laughter. Even if God decides I should be celibate for the next ten years, God forbid, I'm thankful that God will allow me to marry a great man who I can be intimate with. We will be compatible. Thanksgiving doesn't just speak from a place of experience but also from your faith!

IF God doesn't do it, I know He's able! That's not only from experience through a personal relationship, but that's also strength from my faith. This is why the scripture in Philippians goes on to say in verse 7 "And the peace of God, which passeth all understanding, shall keep your hearts and minds through Christ Jesus." Once you have prayed and asked God, and we'll keep it in the context of marriage, for a husband and a blessed union, you can relax.

When you have really established a relationship with God and know who He is for yourself, you can trust that He's heard your prayer. Now you need faith enough to believe that it shall come to pass. Once your faith matches your request, the peace of God will keep you. The peace of God will keep you when you hear that a sister at the church is getting married. The peace of God will keep you when you see a couple in the park on a romantic picnic. The peace of God will keep you when you just have a desire to be held. In that peace, your faith is a reminder that you put your complete trust in God to bring the right man into your life. That man will hold you before you ask him, surprise you with lunch in a picnic basket, will serenade you, comfort you, encourage you, laugh with you, and whatever else you have faith enough to believe God for.

I'm going to be transparent; I know that God is going to bless me with a husband that likes to sing. He might not be able to hold a note, but he'll love to sing. I know this because the one thing I've had faith enough to believe God for in a husband, is man who doesn't mind serenading his wife. I don't need luxury gifts and vacations, although, those are nice. However, I'd rather my husband give me his undivided attention for five minutes to serenade me, than to hand me a blue box and hope I like the bedazzled jewelry inside. In those five minutes, I might get a second round of wedding vows. In those five minutes, he can express his heartfelt appreciation and love toward me. I might forget I got a blue box, but I'd never forget my man singing to me. That's just me! You know what, I anticipate him singing to me. I don't know who my husband is, but I'm excited knowing that he will be just right for me.

I'm not uncertain about one day getting married. I'm getting married one day. I've stopped imagining what my wedding day would be like, and

I've learned to invest more time praying for my husband. That's right. I have no clue what the groom's name is, but I pray for him often. I've gotten to the point that I rarely use "future husband."

See, anticipation is faith at work. You will begin to speak as if you're already married, when your faith has caught up with your request. Occasionally I have to remind myself, "I am somebody's wife!" You are somebody's wife! Say it, "I AM SOMEBODY'S WIFE!" I pray you said it with conviction. If you didn't, I implore you to say it until you've convinced yourself, that you are somebody's wife!

What I love about anticipating my husband is, I'm not concerned about whether he'll be able to meet my expectations, or commonly if I'll be able to meet his. As stated, anticipation is faith at work. If you really have faith in God, you will begin to thank God that your husband will be all that you need him to be. We fear as women what our husbands won't be able to do.

Be honest. I love to laugh and you may love to laugh too. When we meet the right man, of course we hope he'll have a great sense of humor. However, I'm here to tell you to anticipate him having a good sense of humor. Some of us have or will have some demanding careers; therefore, you need to anticipate your husband being supportive. However, don't anticipate your husband being something you yourself are not actually willing to be. I had to slide that in. When he's having a bad day, do you have a sense of humor that can help pull him out of his funk? Will you be supportive when his career begins to skyrocket? Even in your anticipation, don't make yourself solely the recipient.

What do I mean by that? Don't anticipate simply what your husband will be to you, but also anticipate what you will be to your husband. I anticipate my husband serenading me, yes I do, because I'm also saying I anticipate being the apple of my husband eye. I anticipate being my husband's counselor in the sense that I will listen to him as he vents, shares his ideas, and I will offer sound and godly advice when he is teetering in making an important decision. I anticipate on being his favorite masseuse, specializing in foot and back rubs. I truly anticipate on occasion being his special order cook because he's craving my candied yams.

It's silly that we can have faith in an almighty God for healing from cancer and other sicknesses, but we don't have faith enough to believe that same God can bless us in marriage. This is why we become anxious. We don't really trust a holy God to understand what we want.

We don't expect our God to understand that we want to marry someone who can match or outdo our libido. Be honest! As Christians, we feel we shouldn't even think like that. Therefore, we pray for years that God take it, but He hasn't. If you really expect to marry the person God has created for you, you would want to keep the sexual appetite that God has given you. It has purpose! It seems wrong for a holy God to give you a sexual appetite, but sex was created for marriage. It is the world's label and use of sex that has made it seem- well you know- bad! Your appetite is for your marriage. Now if God gave you a healthy libido and He has created only one man specifically for you, wouldn't you think God has also given him a healthy libido? Your prayer shouldn't be for God to take away your libido, but rather that He keeps you and your libido in check!

God knows what you want and He knows what you need. This is why you can anticipate your husband being just right for you. This is why you don't have to make a grocery list of your desires and read it off to God hoping that the man He blesses you with possesses some of those traits.

Put your faith into action. Do whatever preparation you need to do as a woman to be receptive of that right man. I told myself I don't want to have to lose weight before my wedding to shop for a wedding dress. I'm working day by day to get down to my goal weight. I want to be able to go on a two-week honeymoon, or longer to a place of my, okay our choosing. That kind of luxury requires me to save now. However, I have to learn not to spend what I save. I'm an impulsive spender. I go to the store for toilet tissue and walk out of the store with sixty dollars worth of impulse items. It's all things that I need, but not immediately.

Although I've had to postpone furthering my education to raise my daughter, I was never going to stop at my Bachelors. I want to already be back in school working on my medical degree by the time I get married. These are a few things I need to be working on or preparing for while I anticipate my husbands arrival. What about you?

Not only should you physically, emotionally and mentally anticipate his arrival, but also you should be praying for him. There are so many things you can be praying for in regards to your husband including his health, his ministry, his anointing, strength, courage, his faith, and his family. When I pray for my husband, I ask God to surround him with people that will love him and encourage him. I ask God to protect him from the devices of the enemy. I ask God to guard his heart and his mind, and give him peace. I anticipate his arrival so I pray for him!

The truth of the matter is, if you aren't really ready to be married, and I'm speaking not sure if you want to be married, anticipating won't be for you. The other ugly truth is, if you don't trust God, there is no way you can have faith enough to believe that "he is a rewarder of them that diligently seek him." Hebrews 11:6c. Therefore, anticipation doesn't apply to you.

Those who have established a real relationship with God, and have had faith enough to pray for that one man, anticipate! I can't tell you what to anticipate. This whole book is about your personal experience; first your personal experience with God, and secondly the one you will embark upon with your husband. I can't write about what will happen when you meet him. That is a personal experience. Some of you will be skeptical and pray for signs upon signs that he's the one. For some of you, it will be love at first sight. Whatever the case, that's for God to unfold. Simply- anticipate! Get busy for God. Love on Him first, and watch how the story unfolds!

Dear heavenly and most gracious God! Thank you for being all that you are loving and kind. I thank you that you would send a message to love you first! God thank you for desiring to draw closer to us. Help us to take what you've given us, and to make you the first priority in our lives. We want you to be pleased. Now God, each woman who is reading and will read this book, I pray that you bless them. Help them to see themselves as you see them. Allow them to build permanent relationships with you. You know the heart and mind of each individual; touch right now. Help them to relax in you, knowing that you got them. Build their faith in you. Give them those godly attributes, the fruit of your spirit that they may be all that you desire. I bind the enemy that has sought their lives, their ministry, their anointing, their faith, their mind and their soul. Your assignment has been canceled in the name of Jesus! No weapon and no demon you have sent to hinder the plan of God for their lives will prosper. You are ashes under our feet! I declare victory now. I declare peace now. I declare healing now! What you have meant for evil, GOD is turning it around for their good! Hallelujah! God, we thank you for building our faith and trust in you. There is nothing that you will withhold from us when we walk uprightly. Thank you! We love, honor and adore you! In Jesus name, Amen!